DAVID BOUCHARD

with Sally Bender, Anne Letain
and Lucie Poulin-Mackey

For the Love *of* Reading

Books to Build
Lifelong Readers

ORCA BOOK PUBLISHERS

National Library of Canada Cataloguing in Publication Data

Bouchard, David, 1952–
For the love of reading : books to build life long readers / David Bouchard; with Sally Bender, Anne Letain and Lucie Poulin-Mackey.

Includes bibliographical references and index.
ISBN 1-55143-281-1

1. Children's literature — Bibliography. 2. Children — Books and reading. 3. Best books. I. Title.

Z1037.B785 2004   011.62   C2004-900275-9

Library of Congress Control Number: 2004100188

Summary: Lists of children's books for all ages: four experts on literacy share their favorite titles and their best ideas.

Orca Book Publishers gratefully acknowledges the support of its publishing program provided by the following agencies: the Department of Canadian Heritage, the Canada Council for the Arts, and the British Columbia Arts Council.

Design: Timmings & Debay; Cover Image: Getty Images
Printed and bound in Canada

Orca Book Publishers
1030 North Park Street
Victoria, BC Canada
V8T 1C6

Orca Book Publishers
PO Box 468
Custer, WA USA
98240-0468

07 06 05 04 • 4 3 2 1

For teacher-librarians everywhere — that this might assist you in your struggle to promote literacy through good books.

David Bouchard

To the carousel of kids who have passed through my library at St. Patrick's School in Taber, Alberta, and have taught me so much about children and reading.

Anne Letain

For David, Erin and Bret, my partners for the journey.

Sally Bender

To the loves of my life, Paul, Sébastien and Olivier.

Lucie Poulin-Mackey

Introduction

All children should receive the gift of reading, which brings with it access to the world through the written word. And reading is our gift to give. Children are not born wanting to read. They learn from us. We — parents, educators, all adults with children in our lives — must show children the way toward becoming lifelong readers.

We have become addicted to the electronic screen. We have come to believe that we are able to buy most of what we need in our lives. We have developed lifestyles that are not in keeping with good reading practices.

If our children are going to read, we must monitor the use of technology in our homes and schools. And, most important, we must make reading a part of our own lives. No one can do the job for us. No agency, no game, no new curriculum, no magical school can relieve us of our responsibilities. We — parents, teachers and administrators — must all become responsible for our roles in the reading process. We must, each and every one of us, model good reading practices. We must all start reading.

Literacy Canada reports that 54 percent of Canadian adults choose not to read, even though they can. If our children are going to learn to read for the love of it, we must all begin reading for the love of it. And I mean all of us. Has your minister of education read Harry Potter? Do your administrators support and lead in the fight against illiteracy?

We cannot bribe or threaten our children into becoming lifelong readers. They are not going to learn to love reading because of tougher standards or a higher bar. Our kids are going to learn to read for passion when we adults fall under that magical spell. Their fires are going to start to burn if and when they see in us a towering inferno.

Reading holds out to us and to our children access to the greatest range of thought possible. Reading offers all of us access to the world so that we come better to understand ourselves, those around us, history, culture and science. Reading enriches our ability to express our feelings, to question. Our own love for reading allows us to pass on to the next generation that which has been given to us: the gift of reading.

Our reading woes cannot and will not be solved by new and exciting programs, nor will harder-working teachers overcome them. We must seek out that part of our children's hearts that will make them want to read. We must recognize that the key to reaching our children is in modeling. If we want our children to be polite, we must not lecture them on good manners. We need only be polite. If we want our children to read, it is for us to begin reading.

We adults must surround ourselves with our favorite books. We must be seen reading them. We must talk about them. Educators, we must share them with our students. Parents, we must share them with our children. Only through a committed community effort will we be successful.

The premise of the book that precedes this one, *The Gift of Reading*, is that each and every adult with a child in his or her life must read. Each of us must read, collect and share books with the children in our lives. Parents, teachers, administrators, teacher assistants, grandparents . . . we must all read and collect books. In order to light a fire in the hearts of our children, a fire must be burning within our own hearts. We must find the time and courage to ignite our own fires and to stoke them, at all times.

If you are a teacher or an administrator working in a K-8 school, you should build collections including favorites for each age group in your school. If your classroom or office is in the secondary system, your collection should include a variety of books for all reading levels for high-school-aged students.

Your collection must be alive, vibrant and growing!

The key to getting started is to start. Pick up a book and read. Getting started is as simple as that. However, once you've got past that first or second book, then what?

This book will assist you in choosing the third book, the fourth book and many, many more after that. This book is for those who already understand the importance of reading to and with our children. This is for those who want to build or add to their collection of children's books. This is for every teacher, administrator or parent who is seeking ideas and direction as to which books to explore, which books to add to their libraries. This book will help you build a collection that you can call your very own.

I've purposely avoided referring to this as a book that deals with children's books, although you will soon conclude that most of the books my colleagues and I recommend appeal to children.

Books that are meant to engage our youth have traditionally been called children's books, picture books and books for young readers. These labels can interfere with efforts to get ourselves and our kids reading for the love of reading.

Years ago, Walt Disney discovered the key to success in promoting his movies. It was to hook parents and children alike. Disney came to master this art and, in so doing, has taught us something that we can apply to teaching kids to love reading.

Disney spared nothing to draw adults into his world. Disney movies appeal to the entire family. They could be classified as children's movies or movies for young viewers, but they are not. Disney wanted viewers to understand that his movies were meant to be shared. Moms and dads are invited, almost compelled, to sit and watch Disney movies with their children.

For more than half a century, children and adults alike have been hooked on Disney movies. It's time for us to get adults and children hooked on books! The books that my colleagues and I recommend to you appeal to children and to adults. We have made a conscious effort to recommend books that appeal to everyone in the family. Our suggestions are usually books that children, educators and parents can enjoy together.

Individual tastes in reading are as diverse as the music we listen to or the movies that we enjoy. The books that I recommend here are my favorites. Anne Letain recommends her favorites, Sally Bender hers and Lucie Poulin-Mackey hers. You are almost certain to find that one of us has tastes similar to your own. My co-authors have dedicated their lives to children; they know children's books. We have over one hundred years of combined service between us!

In this book, the four of us direct you to books for children of all ages — from birth to adulthood. The lists in this book are for educators and parents alike. Maintaining and adding to our personal libraries must be a lifelong process if our children are going to become lifelong readers.

Seeking out new and exciting books can be tedious and difficult. This book will help. In addition to annotated lists, we have included favorite quotations from some of the books and anecdotes about others, with ideas for how to share them or inspirational stories about experiences we have had. Chapters seven and eight provide lists of seasonal books and some of our favorite resources for choosing books. The last chapter, chapter nine, provides lists of our favorite strategies for sharing the love of reading and the strategies that we think are the most damaging. In that chapter, Anne Letain tells about her Grand Conversations, wildly successful reading groups for children. I think you will find that there is something here for everyone.

I heard about Anne and Sally and Lucie long before I met them. Each of them is legendary in her own community for what she knows and for what she does. Their passion for books is the talk of the town and often spreads across borders to neighboring districts and cities.

Anyone who is anyone in southern Manitoba's literary circle knows the name Sally Bender. Sally is renowned for her love of books and for her obsession with getting kids reading! She is a passionate teacher-librarian and is one of the entrepreneurs who changed a local teacher supply store, Total Teacher, into a children's bookstore that also carries supplies for teachers. She writes a weekly children's book review column for the *Brandon Sun*.

During a tour of southern Alberta a few years ago, I was introduced to Anne Letain, a teacher-librarian and consultant. Anne is the host of a terrific web site called The Read Aloud Registry (www.geocities.com/ aletain). Anne has compiled an extensive list of favorite books and recommended readings of many authors, teachers, politicians, and any who care to share their passion for a good book. She also leads Grand

Conversations, book discussion groups, with the students in her school. The program is voluntary, and Anne can barely keep up with the demand.

Lucie Poulin-Mackey does in the French community in Ontario what Anne and Sally do in their communities in Alberta and Manitoba. She is now the literacy specialist for her school board and shares new authors and new teaching strategies in her ongoing workshops.

Throughout this book, Anne, Sally and I recommend our favorite books in English, and Lucie recommends her favorite books in French. In Canada, nearly one-third of our children are educated in French, either as a mother tongue or in French immersion. With Lucie's lists, the parents and teachers of those children have a ready supply of wonderful books in French.

Each annotation of a Canadian book is marked with a maple leaf to aid readers further in making selections.

Our hope is that educators and parents might find this book a helpful resource. We must never underestimate the value of using our librarians, bookstores and the children we love as our first sources of guidance. That being said, the list that we've put together should help each of you create a collection of your own special favorites — favorites that will allow you and your children or students to become lovers of reading.

For years now, I have kept in constant contact with Sally, Anne and Lucie; they never cease to direct me to books, new and old, that I must read. Together, we will help you compile a collection of your very own.

Happy reading!

Finding the Books

Whether you are looking for books in French or in English, we recommend that you start with your local bookstore, the children's bookstore if there is one in your community. Get to know your local bookstore owner; befriend him or her. That person will be your most important ally. If you work in a school, your teacher-librarian will be an equally important person in your life, a person with the knowledge and skills to find the books that you want. You may also wish to visit book fairs sponsored by local schools or order books from book club flyers that are sent to schools every month. Many publishers also have a web site from which you may place orders. For those titles that are more difficult to find, you can contact a book wholesaler that specializes in titles for schools. In western Canada, United Library Services is a great place to contact, while in eastern Canada there are several wholesalers including National Book Service and S&B Books. A wholesaler can also offer significant discounts to purchasers.

If you are looking for French books outside the French areas of Canada, you may need to go farther afield, although if you are armed with an author and a title, you will be able to order many French books through your local bookstore if you cultivate the relationship. For those harder-to-find titles, you might consider joining a book club such as Quebec Loisirs. Or you could visit the web site of a major bookstore in Quebec such as Renauld-Bray or Archambault. You will not receive unless you ask. Be patient, smile, and before you know it your personal library will be completed with newfound treasures.

CHAPTER ONE

Pre-conception to Two

Part 1: *David Bouchard*

The attitude of parents and teachers toward reading is the single most important factor in providing children with the gift of reading.

My first list, books that I recommend for parents of babies, includes both wonderful books for babies and books that provide adults with insight into some important issues that relate to learning to read. While some books are particularly well suited to newborns and toddlers, the most important thing is that parents make reading aloud a priority. At this age, children don't care what is being read to them. They need their mom and dad to sit with them, to share their space, to look into their eyes, to breathe down upon them. Read *A Story for Bear* first. This gentle story expresses all the reasons to read to our children from the moment they are born.

Among the titles in this list, I've suggested books that remind us what some have sacrificed that they might come to read and write. Read *Nightjohn* now, for your child and for yourself. Come to know how truly fortunate we are to have access to "the letters." Read *Nightjohn* again when your child is older and ready to appreciate our good fortune.

For a taste of the obstacles different children will have to face as they grow, read *Knots on a Counting Rope* and *Thank You, Mr. Falker.* Read them now and keep them. These are books that are sure to become favorites. I recommend that you share them with your children again at a later date.

For a look at the power that we have as teachers, both for good and ill, read *Changing Places.*

This list is for you, as an educator or as a parent. These are all books that you should read and own. You will want to share these books with your family, friends and neighbors. I can't imagine anyone reading *Reading with Dad* and not rushing out to purchase several copies to hand out to others.

These are all books that you will want to read, own and share. And sharing is a passion right at the heart of reading.

Denton, Kady MacDonald (Illustrator)
A Child's Treasury of Nursery Rhymes ❀

I am horrified to think that a child could grow up without the gift of nursery rhymes. However, it does happen. I feel an emptiness deep within when my wife shares these beautiful nursery rhymes with our daughter, Victoria. I cannot share them in the same way, as I never heard any as a child. Who better to illustrate these favorites than Canada's own Denton? A spectacular book!

> Sally Bender first shared this book with us. She and I had just met and discovered our mutual love of books. Sally wanted to begin a relationship with our daughter, Victoria, through books. The first book that she chose to send was Kady MacDonald Denton's *Treasury*. She knew that we would have many books of nursery rhymes, but this one is very special to her. She and Kady are friends, and she was captivated by Kady's artwork, as we were too when we received the book. What better way to reach out to a new friend's child than through a beloved book?

Dhami, Narinder *Changing Places*

Our children often come to believe what others believe about them. This reality is cleverly portrayed in Dhami's *Changing Places* and can be a valuable tool to you as you attempt to turn children into readers. Surround your children with books. Get them their own membership at the local library. Set up an account for them at a local bookstore. Paper their bedrooms with wallpaper that looks like a library. Visitors to your children's world will pick up on their intimacy with books and reading. Your children's friends will come to believe that they are readers. And your children will come to see themselves as readers. This isn't the only way, but it is a clear step in the right direction.

In *Changing Places*, an enrolling thug is somehow confused with an enrolling straight-A student who arrives at school on the same day. It takes little time for each boy to learn to live up to what is expected from him.

Haseley, Dennis *A Story for Bear*

This is a book about a woman who reads to a bear. She and her bear develop a reading relationship, but Bear can't read. Bear can't understand a single word that is read to him. Why would anyone suggest "a story for bear" or, in our world, "a story for baby"? The answer brooks no argument in this beautifully illustrated treasure. You will want to own it and then you'll want to share.

> *The bear gazed up at her as she said the words and turned the pages. He couldn't understand any of what she was saying. But as he listened to the sound of her voice, happiness washed over him like waves.*

Heide, Florence Parry *The Problem with Pulcifer*

We understand how harmful television can be if not controlled and yet, in the majority of our homes, we do not succeed in keeping it in its proper place. Heide uses a twist in her tale to remind us of our roles in keeping the television in check. In this charming little book, Pulcifer is unlike other children in that he prefers reading to watching television. The adults in the story have their work cut out for them as they try to make him conform.

Hoberman, Mary Ann *You Read to Me and I'll Read to You*

This book is a compilation of language and thoughts that speak to the importance of reading to and with those you love. As the title suggests, this gentle read will be one that you will use often with your young ones. You'll appreciate the rhythm and rhyme as well as the fun illustrations in this addition to your collection.

Jorgensen, Richard *Reading with Dad*

This is a delightful picture book somewhat similar to *Love You Forever*. Like the Munsch classic, it follows a parent and child through life, in this case a daughter and her father. It highlights the best times in a little girl's life — all times when she was reading with Dad. I've shared this touching book with hundreds of thousands over the past few years. I can't tell you how many people it brought to tears. I am among those who have never known the pleasure of having my father (or my mother) read to me. However, my daughter will not fall into that group.

Don't even think about buying only one copy of this classic. You'll need dozens. You will, as I have done, want to share the power and responsibility we have in reading to our children with all those you love. Have a box of tissues handy. You'll need it. I have read this book to tens of thousands at conferences across North America. If you've heard me speak, you've likely heard me read *Reading with Dad*.

Longfellow, Henry *Poetry for Young People*

Poetry is important to all children. It is particularly valuable for those whose strengths might not lie in reading. Poetry offers its readers many routes to enjoyment and understanding. Rhythm and rhyme are tools that we can all use as we learn to read. This series, which includes collections of poetry by Shakespeare, Emily Dickinson, and Robert Louis Stevenson, is amazing. Very nicely illustrated.

Martin, Bill, Jr. and John Archambault
Knots on a Counting Rope

Bill Martin Jr. is an amazing author — one of the best of our era. This touching book reminds us of how important it is that we learn to believe in ourselves and in those we love. A young, blind, First Nations boy learns to see through his darkness. Guiding him are his grandparents, two blue horses and the power of stories, each and every one recorded on the knots of his grandfather's counting rope. Witness the magic of a beautifully illustrated book and the pleasure of a child who is proud and happy with who he is, despite being blind. Do not read this one without tissues at hand.

This book depicts an elder, a grandfather who ties a knot in a rope every time he tells his grandson a story. The old man keeps count of his tellings, of the tales he shares . . . stories that highlight traditions, values and beliefs.

I knew a teacher who read this book to her class and then introduced them, ceremonially, to what was going to be their own counting rope. She and her students tied a knot in their rope after each story that they shared together. The rope was always proudly displayed and shared with visitors.

McBratney, Sam *Guess How Much I Love You*

This touching little picture book about a bunny and his loving mother is another must for every child's library. It is also a must for parents. The illustrations are amazing. The simple message cuts to the quick. Get it early in your collecting. Write both your name and your child's in it.

Milne, A.A. *When We Were Very Young*

My wife, Vicki, would never forgive me if I didn't include her all-time favorite as a child. This charming book of gentle, childhood poems is perhaps the classic of all classics. Add it to your collection and work at mastering Milne's amazing poems. Read them again and again until you've made them your own. Read them to your babies until the day they leave home. Then give it to them to take away with them.

Munsch, Robert *Love You Forever* ❧

This million-book seller is for mothers. It is a chronological look at the life of a parent and a child, depicted through the eyes of a loving mother and then her son. Read it to a grade one class and you'll find children in the aisles, laughing. Read it to their mothers and you'll see laughter replaced with tears.

Paulsen, Gary *Nightjohn*

Gary Paulsen is one of my favorite authors. *Nightjohn* takes place in the far south during the age of slavery and tells the story of a young girl who desperately wants to learn to read. It speaks of the sacrifices of her teacher, Nightjohn, and the sacrifices that were made in order that children might be given the gifts of reading and writing. Paulsen reminds us of our good fortune in "knowing our letters." Read *Nightjohn* and keep it for later. You will want to share it again with your child when she turns twelve.

Polacco, Patricia *Thank You, Mr. Falker*

Mr. Falker is the teacher we all want our children to have. Patricia Polacco tells her personal story, that of a young dyslexic girl who had tremendous difficulty learning to read . . . until Mr. Falker came into her life. Though this success story is, sadly, not the norm for most learning disabled children, it doesn't prevent us from celebrating it and from striving for something just like it with each of our children.

Wangerin, Walter, Jr. *The Bedtime Rhyme*

I love the way Americans enjoy mush in their books and in their movies. Americans seem to love to cry. This touching, well-illustrated poem of a grandfather speaking to his grandchild of the love deep in his heart might not move you to tears, but it will, without doubt, move you to hug your babies while muttering, "That's just the way Daddy feels about you, darling!" I love reading this book to my daughter. Four Hearts!

Wells, Rosemary *Read to Your Bunny*

Rosemary Wells offers us a perfectly sweet book. Read to your babies and they will soon be reading to their teddies, their dolls and . . . their bunnies.

Zelinsky, Paul *The Wheels on the Bus*
(with parts that move)

Young children should all be privy to the magic of story and song together. *The Wheels on the Bus* is a picture book that allows you to sing your way through the classic children's song. It will captivate young children and will turn mediocre adult readers into master readers. Make this book one of your favorites. This particular version is special in the way it sounds, looks and feels.

Part II: *Anne Letain*

When I saw all my selections put together and annotated, I realized that I had been working toward a single principle that I hold dear to my heart!

After many years of teaching, it has become obvious to me that children today are coming to school ill-prepared for the reading experience. We can blame it on busy lives, on television or whatever, but too many of today's children come to school lacking the oral essentials and language they need to kick-start the love of reading.

These are some of the books that I would choose to put the oral language tradition back into the reading experience. You will see copious Mother Goose, lots of old stories and songs presented in unusual ways, plenty of repetition and silliness, and frequent opportunities for lap-time and sharing between parent and child. There are only three linear stories here — chosen for their simplicity and for their relationship to the real-life experience of the very young child. These fifteen gems are my foundation choices for a lifetime of reading.

Barton, Byron *The Little Red Hen*

Byron Barton is a perennial top pick with and for the very young. This is a simple retelling of an old favorite. The language and the imaginative graphics make this version an obvious choice for a first childhood exposure to the tale of the independent red hen who feeds her family without any help from her lazy friends.

Brown, Marc Tolon (Illustrator) *Hand Rhymes*

Marc Brown has gathered together fourteen hard-to-find rhymes that are usually performed with hand actions (such as "Here Is the Church"). A noted illustrator, his pictorial representations for performing the poems are perfect — even for the hand/eye challenged. Some are classic finger rhymes. Some are new. The follow-up book, *Finger Rhymes*, would also be an excellent companion and purchase.

Brown, Margaret Wise *Goodnight Moon*

This is the classic bedtime book, surprisingly so in that the illustrations are not outstanding and the verse is sort of silly. In the book, a wee rabbit tries to put off bedtime by saying goodnight to all the objects in his bedroom. Young children are entranced and lulled by the rhythm of this small story and beg for it over and over again. Although there are many related *Goodnight Moon* products available on the market today, a best bet would be the companion book *The Runaway Bunny*.

Burns, Kate *Blink Like an Owl*

Part of a quartet of flap-books including *Snap Like a Crocodile*, *Waddle Like a Duck* and *Jump Like a Frog*, *Blink Like an Owl* asks children animal-related questions and offers the answers under a flap. But there's a bonus. Under each flap, kids are invited to mimic each animal in a particular way, for example, "to blink like an owl." The illustrations are particularly colorful, but it's the "let's pretend" that makes these books valuable to own.

> I usually haven't even handed out the ground rules when I'm presenting Kate Burns' *Blink Like an Owl* before the whole library turns into the Calgary Zoo. There's stretching, waddling, growling, hooting—you name it. They can hardly wait for me to turn the page so that they can move on to the next action or noise. Of course, it's so bad that I have to make sure both library doors are shut. I usually do two books from the series at a time, and believe me, on the following week nobody lets me forget that there are two more books left to do.

Clarke, Gus (Illustrator)
EIEIO: The Story of Old MacDonald, Who Had a Farm

An original and witty version of the traditional song, *EIEIO* is utterly appealing. A hilarious cast of characters engages in activities that culminate in a humorous surprise ending. The book provides endless opportunities for children to chime in and join the fun.

Degen, Bruce *Jamberry*

Jamberry has to be one of the most imaginative books ever conceived for infants and young children. The rhyming is delectable and careens through the book with the speed of a runaway train. Children clamor to climb on board with the boy and the berry-loving bear in search of more fruit. To be enjoyed over and over again for both the words and the magnificent illustrations. It's Razzmatazzberry!

Ellwand, David (Illustrator)
Clap Your Hands: An Action Book

Gifted photographer David Ellwand has turned that classic old song "If You're Happy and You Know It" into an oversized board book for toddlers. Featuring a bevy of gorgeous teddy bears (old and young) clapping their hands, touching their toes and more, this book will remind readers of all ages just how much fun being happy (and knowing it) is.

Hughes, Shirley *Alfie Gets in First*

The very first in the Alfie series, *Alfie Gets in First* tells the story of toddler Alfie, who gets home first on foot from a shopping trip and promptly manages to lock his mother and baby sister, Annie Rose, out of the house. Soon the whole neighborhood is frantically trying to restore Alfie to his family. There's a happy and predictable ending, of course. Hughes has a remarkable talent for portraying ordinary life situations in a way that everyone (child and adult alike) can relate to.

Lottridge, Celia Barker *Mother Goose: A Sampler* ❈

Twenty-eight of Canada's best illustrators for children donated their time and talent to this outstanding collection of Mother Goose rhymes selected by Celia Lottridge (noted storyteller and founder of the Parent-Child Mother Goose Program in Canada). The format is impeccable as each nursery rhyme is portrayed with a two-page spread of print and illustration — each poem standing on its own and no conflict of style between illustrators.

Opie, Iona *My Very First Mother Goose*
and *Here Comes Mother Goose*

There are Mother Goose books and there are Mother Goose books, but these are definitely the ones to buy! Iona Opie is a world-renowned folklorist, and the selected verses are just right for the infant and preschool set. Combine these wonderful choices with Rosemary Wells' humorous and quirky illustrations and you've got a surefire hit. Each book includes an index of first lines for the parent who just can't remember that particular rhyme.

Raffi *Down by the Bay* ✤

This pictorial rendition of the classic song is a keeper. Now available as a board book, *Down by the Bay* will become a much-loved and asked-for read aloud. In no time at all it will be memorized, and the kids will be making their own rhymes to compete with "a bear combing his hair" or "a goose kissing a moose." The illustrations are terrific too! It's also a perfect vehicle for teachers to use for initial writing experiences.

Reid, Barbara *Zoe's Sunny Day* ✤

Reid's quartet of board books, which also includes *Zoe's Snowy Day*, *Zoe's Rainy Day* and *Zoe's Windy Day*, has recently been republished. This time the formerly wordless books contain a few lines of print that answer the question "Where is Zoe going?" In each book Zoe ventures off into the world (and weather) and then returns to the security of home. Reid's famous plasticine illustrations, complete with trademark detail, compel the reader to return again and again for more examination and discussion.

Shaw, Charles G. *It Looked Like Spilt Milk*

Such a simple concept — a white silhouetted shape on a blue background that changes on each page. Is it a bird or a rabbit or spilt milk? Children are kept guessing right to the surprise ending. This "oldie but goodie" is timeless and presents many possibilities for imagination, talk and creative thought. Very young children will soon be able to "read" this book to their parents with no difficulty.

Wells, Rosemary *Max's Chocolate Chicken*

It's a tough job to figure out which of the Max books is the best, but *Max's Chocolate Chicken* must be near the top of the list. Max (the bunny) and his bossy older sister, Ruby, are on an Easter egg hunt. Ruby naturally pursues the eggs with due diligence, while Max gets distracted by ants and acorns. But, as usual, justice prevails, Max triumphs and gets the chocolate chicken. The illustrations are almost as delicious as the chocolate.

"No eggs, no chicken!" Ruby warns Max.

Wood, Audrey and Don *Piggies*

Don't be tempted to buy anything but the full-sized version of Piggies so that parent and kid can both savor Don Wood's amazing finger pigs. In this inventive and whimsical story, four fingers and a thumb become amazing little piggies with personality on an interesting journey to bedtime. Hand play at its finest.

> *Piggies* is a delight every time I present it. I own a wonderful glove with pigs on the fingers that depicts the "This little piggy goes to market" poem. So first I pull out the glove and we do the first set of pigs. Then I dig out the big yellow *Piggies* book, and I do the first run-through. The second time, the kids get to say it with me and try to join their fingers together in sequence! When they leave I test them on their "piggies," and they must raise the correct finger and identify the name of that particular piggy (like the Wee Piggy). Boy, it's tough getting up a couple of those fingers and keeping the rest of them down at the same time. And it's too much fun! The book is so popular that it's worn out on a regular basis from all the circulation.

Part III: *Sally Bender*

As young parents, my husband and I were not aware of the lifelong effect that our reading aloud would have on our children. But we read all the time ourselves and so we read to our kids. We read aloud whatever we were reading as we rocked our children and sat with them in those early days and months. I know that is why Erin and Bret still read *Sports Illustrated* every week. They often heard stories from that magazine in their dad's voice, always gentle and quiet.

I read newspapers, novels and magazines, and I read them all out loud. I followed Bret around the house reading to him. He was so busy that he didn't have time to sit still, and I was worried that he was missing the joy that we had shared with Erin as she sat fascinated by our voices and the words. We sang all the time and shared nursery rhymes from our childhood every chance that we got. The books that I chose for this section reflect the young child's love of rhyme and rhythm and recognizable repetitive text.

Alexander, Martha *A You're Adorable*

Singing songs to your baby is such a spontaneous ritual; those songs may come from a long history of singing in your family or from some of the wonderful songbooks that have been developed with young listeners in mind.

When Martha Alexander decided to illustrate a traditional song, she did us all a favor. She took words that many of us know and love and created a book to be enjoyed by new generations. *A You're Adorable* is an alphabet book inspired by good feelings and filled with images of multiracial toddlers in unframed and uncluttered artwork.

Boynton, Sandra *Moo, Baa, La, La, La!*

Kids love to make the sounds that farm animals make, and they like it even more when we mix up those sounds. Sandra Boynton has used that premise in a rhythmic ode to the animals that young children love to imitate. Of course, she has her three little pigs totally out of sync with the rest of the text.

This book will surely lead you to the others in the series of eight board books for the very young. Filled with fun and frivolity, they touch on such concepts as the alphabet, opposites, colors and bedtime rituals.

Brown, Ruth *Ten Seeds*

Ruth Brown's detailed and realistic illustrations bring to life this informative and innovative counting book. It all begins with ten seeds and one ant. The ant has planted the seeds in verdant soil, teeming with earthworms and the nutrients that all seeds need for growth. As the counting progresses, we note that many things can happen to planted seeds. They send down roots and sprout shoots. They also fall prey to a variety of natural enemies. In the end, if we are lucky, those ten seeds will produce one plant that will, in turn, give back ten seeds.

Much learning will accompany the sharing of this delightfully simple concept book, which is told in forty-five words. Pair this book with its companion, *Snail Trail*, for a generous helping of what can happen in a garden.

Fleming, Denise *Mama Cat Has Three Kittens*

In this brilliantly illustrated book, we meet Mama Cat and her three young kittens. Two of them do as they are expected to, but not Boris. While Mama Cat and Boris's siblings are doing what cats do, Boris is napping. We watch as they go about the business of their day, and, in each case, Boris is caught doing what he does best. When Mama, Fluffy and Skinny need a nap after their busy day, Boris is more than ready to use the energy he has stored while catnapping.

The beautifully bright illustrations are textured and detailed. The expressions on the faces of the cats will have children recognizing just what they are thinking as they try to deal with their errant family member. With its patterned and repetitive text and its surprise ending, this book is perfect for encouraging a love of reading.

Fox, Mem *Boo to a Goose*

Mem Fox creates books that introduce young children to the beauty of our language. She works endlessly to choose just the right word and to tell a pleasing tale fit for all readers and listeners. Her many books lead to hours of lively and lovely conversation.

Boo to a Goose is filled with descriptive, rhythmic language that introduces such words as Kalamazoo, piranhas, bellow and Calcutta. Each two-line stanza ends with the same refrain: "I wouldn't say 'Boo!' to a goose." Only on the last page do we learn about the event that has led to such wisdom.

Frazee, Marla *Hush, Little Baby*

In the initial illustration for this book, we are introduced to the family whose baby will inspire the actions that finally lead to rest and relaxation. We also come to recognize the tinker man who trades endlessly to find the perfect item to lull the baby to sleep. And, if we are watching closely, we will notice the sister whose constantly changing expressions leave us with no doubt as to what she is thinking.

The sleeping baby is getting a lot of attention that should perhaps be directed elsewhere, and it isn't long before that sleep is disturbed by a jealous onlooker. Then the race is on to calm the baby. It takes much patience and skill to find the just-right solution.

This book presents another traditional song whose words will soon be learned. A reader is born!

Hoban, Tana *Shapes, Shapes, Shapes*

When I first saw Tana Hoban's beautiful photographs, I was amazed at her vision. She takes the most common elements of our world and creates photographs that inspire and intrigue. Her concept books run the gamut from color, shape and size to shadows, geometry and money. In looking at her many books, we have much to learn and to discuss.

In *Shapes, Shapes, Shapes*, she reminds her readers about the shapes that they might look for in the text. Then she takes us out into the world to have a close look at things. A sailboat, a fire truck, the curves and windows on a heritage house, a hopscotch game and a bundle of rattan baskets — all show us the shapes that are right at hand, the shapes that we might not notice if we are not using our "lookers."

Meyers, Susan *Everywhere Babies*

I am always on the lookout for a new baby book, one that I will give to my friends who are having children of their own, or grandbabies (that has to do with my age). I love this wonderful, expressive book about the world of babies. It tells us on the first page about the types of babies that are born every day, everywhere. They range from fat and thin to summer and fall. And then we are on our way to looking at them as they captivate the world. No matter what they are doing, babies hold us in the palms of their hands. We watch as they are kissed, dressed and fed, as they play games, crawl and walk.

The illustrator, Marla Frazee, has filled the pages of *Everywhere Babies* with a sparkling array of babies and toddlers, all grabbing our attention and our hearts.

Every day, everywhere, babies are kissed — on their

*cheeks, on their ears, their fingers, their nose, on the
top of their head, on their tummy, their toes.*

Raffi *Shake My Sillies Out* ❦

When our kids were young, Raffi was a much-loved entertainer. We
had all of his cassettes, and we sang with and danced to his music on a
daily basis. Ten years later, when I was working at the bookstore in my
spare time, I found that he had put his songs into book form, in a series
called "Songs to Read." They were designed to help eager young listeners become familiar with the words and the workings of story. They
remain in print today and continue to help children believe that they
are quite brilliant when they can quickly "read" them. And children are
quick to share that learning.

Shake My Sillies Out is filled with movement and humor. Kids in
need of a break will shake, wiggle, jump and clap their way through it
while using some of their endless store of contained energy. This is one
of a series of ten songs, each special in its own way and sure to please
your young music fan.

Rathmann, Peggy *Good Night, Gorilla*

No matter how often I read this book to my kindergarten kids, they
want to hear it again. Once you have read it, you will want to do the
same thing. It is a simple concept, but the characters are engaging and
their leader is charming.

As the zookeeper says goodnight to each animal in the zoo, only
the reader knows the gorilla's secret. My kids try so hard not to tell!
Once the animals have been released to follow the zookeeper home, it
is left to us to watch his wife be surprised by a gaggle of goodnights.
Her reaction is just what we would expect, and soon the animals are
being led back to their cages in the zoo. Only the gorilla and the mouse
can outsmart her one more time!

Schwartz, Roslyn *The Mole Sisters* series ❦

Eight tiny treasures for preschoolers, these books will delight with their
spirit of adventure and their independent cast of characters. The Mole

Sisters are the endearing duo that graces the pages of each lively quest. They ask questions, try new directions for their meanderings, explore untried territory and go quietly and confidently about all new learning. They are independent and assertive. They are intelligent and resourceful. They are great role models for those who share these books.

Each new volume sparks another quest for information. The Mole Sisters go gathering with panache and are inspired by all that they discover. You will love them and so will your little ones.

Walsh, Ellen Stoll *Mouse Paint*

Somehow, animals make stories more memorable for kids. The three mice in this elegant little jewel of a book are sure to be remembered long after we have shared their story. One day while the cat is away, the mice decide to play. They discover three jars of paint, each containing one of the primary colors. They then decide that those jars are perfect for painting mice.

You can imagine the discoveries that they make while covered with paint and exploring the puddles that have spilled out onto the floor. It is amazing to watch. They end the book by sharing what they have learned, including the warning that you should always leave some white space for white mice, especially when the cat is near.

I always use this book when I want to talk with kids about the joys of mixing colors. Prior to the reading I have provided the three primary colors at the paint table on numerous occasions and let the children make discoveries on their own. It is surprising how often they recognize the principle of mixing two colors, or more, to create another one. When we share the book they are able to project their own experiences with color mixing to the adventures of the mice.

One particular day we had read the book and were proceeding with small paint jars to reenact the story. The mice were chosen and the paraphernalia prepared and the rereading had begun. The red mouse had danced in yellow, and the beauty of the orange that he had created was most impressive. The yellow mouse had danced in blue, and we were agog at the brilliance of the green. When the blue mouse danced into the red paint, he knocked it clear off the table and was heard to exclaim, "Oh, my gosh! Now I've done it. Hey! That author was right . . . blue and red make purple . . . even on the carpet!" Our carpet sports that stain to this day, and the kids in grade four who are partnered with my children this year repeat the whole story time after time as they visit the classroom for partner reading.

Walter, Virginia *Hi, Pizza Man!*

Now here is a book that will have your child reading quickly. It is filled with all things to love . . . the sounds of animals, dinosaurs and a laugh a minute. We begin with Vivian, a hungry little girl who is trying to wait patiently for a pizza to be delivered. While they wait, Mom asks what she will say when it arrives. Vivian decides that she will say "hi" to the pizza man. Thus begins a wildly inventive romp with language and loud laughter. What if it isn't a pizza man? What if it is a pizza woman? A pizza cow? What would you say then?

The pattern of the text and the dialogue that passes between Vivian and the messengers is full of fun and so lively that children will want to hear it again and again . . . and soon they will be telling this story on their own to anyone who will listen.

Every year this story is on our list of "old favorites" from its first reading. It is so appealing to the children's spirit, so filled with fun. For days after reading it, they greet visitors and anyone who will listen with the endless refrain: "Nice to see you at school today, Pizza Principal!" "Let's go home, Pizza Mom!" "Freeze, Pizza Gym Teacher!" "Sing, Pizza Music Teacher!" "Get out of my way, Pizza Brother!"

We use the idea to write our own class book. We go on for pages, with a wild assortment of unique and inane greetings to everyone and everything that comes to mind or into our line of vision.

Imagine the children's surprise when they arrived at school early for one of our noon-hour food events. There we were, seated at the picnic tables and ready for our food, when a pizza deliveryman arrived with piping hot pizzas for lunch. The immediate and delighted response to his arrival was a unanimous chant, "Hi, Pizza Man!" They were so proud.

Williams, Vera *"More, More, More," Said the Baby*

Three sweet love stories about Little Guy, Little Pumpkin and Little Bird are told in this Caldecott Honor book created by the talented and insightful Vera Williams. In each case we are introduced to the baby who will be coddled and cuddled and caught up in the hugs of a daddy, a grandma and a mama. The kisses land on the belly button, the toes and the nose, but in each case they bring squeals of delight and a feeling of contentment to the baby, always asking for more.

Bright, bordered illustrations filled with movement and vibrant color provide the backdrop for this tale of unconditional love. The final segment serves as a story just right for bedtime. Mmm. Mmm. Mmm.

Part IV: *Lucie Poulin-Mackey*

This is your child's first encounter with books. This first list includes books that appeal to all the senses so children can touch them, taste them, smell them, hear them and by all means start to read them. The earlier you start, the better the chance your children have to become early readers and maintain their motivation as they grow older. I remember putting cardboard books in my boys' playpen and plastic books in their bath. The books in this list are all about the experiences your young child is likely to have: first words, bath time and a visit to the zoo, for example.

Bour, Danièle *7 histoires câlines de Petit Ours Brun*

Petit Ours Brun is a character in the popular French kids' magazines *Popi* and *Pomme d'api*. Here, seven stories have been combined to make a very thick book indeed. This simple character enjoys adventures with Mom, Dad and music. He also plays with friends, but it's not always fun. Petit Ours Brun potty trains and has fun with shoes of all shapes and sizes. The young child will learn basic life skills with Petit Ours Brun. Written in simple text and illustrated in bold colors, this book will be enjoyed by all children.

Courtin, Thierry (Illustrator) *T'choupi joue avec l'eau*

T'choupi is a loveable character. Not unlike Caillou or Toupie, T'choupi finds adventure everywhere. In this particular story, T'choupi finds water to play in. He explores, splashes, waters plants and helps his toy to get washed. This is a fun book for bath time. The illustrations are simple and colorful.

Denan, Pierre *Trucs à sentir*

Hold your noses, it's going to stink. Yes, this book describes the smells that fill our lives: good smells, bad smells, sweet smells, smells from the kitchen, outside smells, even personal smells. The pictures are a mixture of real photographs and cartoon characters. A perfect book to help young minds develop language about their senses. A series of questions at the end guides parents or other adults in helping children retrieve information from the book. A good book to read aloud.

Éditions Caramel *Mon tout premier imagier*

Ready, set, go! Are you ready for language development? This is the book for you. It provides over 125 illustrated words in sixteen themes that are relevant to the child's environment, including clothes, food, animals, games and toys. The illustrations are bold and bright. This board book will soon become your child's favorite.

Éditions Korrigan *Gaston le caneton*

Gaston goes on an adventure exploring his surroundings, wading through the water. He meets a friendly frog and they play hide-and-seek. Imagine a green frog in a marsh. Can Gaston find her? He looks everywhere. The child is drawn into the story by the vivid pictures. A surprise for all is reserved for the end. You can imagine the laughs already.

Hastings, Jack *Je suis au zoo*
French text by Rachel Albanese

A trip to the zoo, anyone? This book helps children learn zoo animal names. The photographs that accompany the text show real-life animals, not cartoons. It includes simple text and pictures your child will want to look at over and over again.

Jolin, Dominique *L'Halloween de Toupie* 🍁

Toupie is a lovable mouse whose best friend is a cat. The two pair up in various adventures that sometimes get them in trouble. In this story Toupie helps his best friend, Binou, get dressed for Halloween. A cat in a pumpkin suit is a rare sight indeed! Imagine a big mouse trying to dress a small cat. What an adventure! Through her Toupie series, Dominique Jolin explores several themes dear to the hearts of both adults and children, such as emotions, play, sharing, friendship and so much more. Her illustrations tell the story.

You will find many books in her Galipette collection and also her Chatouille collection. These board books are easy to handle. The language is simple and is written in short sentences that help the child acquire vocabulary. A cute Toupie doll is also available. A must for your child's library.

> We love stories about mice, and for us, Toupie and Binou were beloved characters. My boys would wait anxiously for the next adventure. Since Hallowe'en is my husband's favorite holiday, you should see our house. Christmas is barren compared to Hallowe'en. Not surprising that *L'Halloween de Toupie* quickly became a favorite!

Larranaga, Ana (Illustrator) *Des oreilles pour entendre*

Ears of all shapes, sizes and colors are the stars of this book. The child will be able to flip through and guess whom the ears belong to, the elephant, the monkey or the baby. This bold, shaped board book is easy to handle. The guessing game helps the child develop literacy skills. A great book to cuddle up with on the couch. Other books are available in the series.

Louchard, Antonin *Mon petit cœur*

This book is filled with the loving names we call our children (my cutie pie, my sunshine). These very French expressions remind us of our own childhood. The illustrations humorously reflect the names given. For example, my little chickadee is a chick.

Oxenbury, Helen (creator of series) *Léo et Popi sur le pot*
French text by Claire Clément

Toilet training, anyone? Here's a book to help you and your child with this rite of passage. Léo carries his friend Popi everywhere he goes, into the kitchen, the living room and all over the house. Léo follows Mom into the living room where he sits on his potty. It's much easier to train while talking to your best friend. EUREKA! Success at last. This book is written in simple text, and the pictures tell the story. Other Léo and Popi adventures support various themes related to personal development including eating, bath time and day care.

Powell, Richard and Steve Cox *Qui se cache à la ferme ?*

Peek-a-boo! Where are you? Peek-a-boo! Who are you? This is an illustrated flap-book that will draw the child into a guessing game. Who's hiding in the barn? An animal that begins with the letter C. The rhyming scheme and the bold letters will help the child develop language and also help with literacy skills.

Randell, Beverly, Jenny Giles and Annette Smith *Moi*
French text by Thérèse Mercarder and Martine Mamo-Morel

A book about me. What more can a child ask for? This simple text accompanied by real photographs helps the child deal with emotions. I cry. I smile. And more. This is a good anytime story.

Sarazin, Joceline *Caillou : L'ours en peluche* ✤

Caillou's favorite toy is his teddy bear, Octave. He carries Octave everywhere. He plays with him; he eats with him. When he's hurt, only Octave can console him. One day, Octave is nowhere to be found. The house is turned upside down. Mom even calls Grandma to see if Octave is there. How will Caillou cope? It's dodo time and no bear. Caillou will never sleep without his friend. Dad tries to console him with another toy. "No, Daddy, bunny will never do. I want my bear !!!!!!!" It's no use. Will Caillou ever find his bear? One day Grandma pays a visit. Guess what she's brought with her?

Smith, Annette, Jenny Giles and Beverly Randell *Bébé*
French text by S. de Joncas

This is one of a beautiful collection of books. The simple text is accompanied by photographs. This one speaks to the child directly, showing things baby does during the day and during the night. Baby eats. Baby cries. And finally baby sleeps. At least we hope that baby sleeps.

Zanimo (Fabienne Michot et Doris Brasset)
Maki je suis content ✤

Maki is a lemur from Madagascar who is both exotic and colorful. These books reflect the "me" that is so important in a child's being. The authors strive to offer a positive and stimulating environment to young minds, encompassing self-confidence and the beauty of discovering the world. Simple text and easy vocabulary help in the acquisition of language and simple notions. Some of this team's books have been finalists for the Mr. Christie Award.

CHAPTER TWO

Three- to Five-Year-Olds

Part I: *David Bouchard*

Unlike my previous list, where many of my recommendations were directed at adults, this list is for children. Let it be clear, however, that parental/adult involvement is the single most important factor in turning our children into lifelong readers.

The books that you choose together with your children must appeal to you as well as to them. You must collect books that you enjoy or you risk having your fire die out. Your enthusiasm for these books will shine through all you do and say. When you go to the movies with someone, you talk about your likes and dislikes. You usually end up going to one you both like. Good children's books are available in great numbers. Be sure to choose books that appeal to your children and to you.

It is in this age group that you will find the greatest selection of picture books. Of the twenty books on my list, nineteen are picture books. I could have listed two hundred, as there are so many on the market. Your task will be to collect a variety and to learn to discriminate in your choice of writing styles and messages.

You will want some books written in rhythm and rhyme. You'll want some in prose. Seek out books that speak to your culture and family values. Look for others that aim at something higher, something more global (i.e., *The Giving Tree*). Certain messages in children's books transcend any one country, culture or religion.

Children at this age will, to varying degrees, want to become involved in the reading process. Do not rush them. Let them progress at their own speeds. Some, like my Victoria, will love finishing the verses in books that are written in rhythm and rhyme (i.e., *Petite Rouge*). Others, possibly as early as five-year-olds, will take the books from your hands and begin reading themselves. You are not reading to and with your children to get them into Harvard (Alfie Kohn describes this parental hang-up as "Preparation H"). We are not teaching our children to read to help them pass tests. We are not reading with them so that they can achieve more and more quickly. We are reading with those we love in order to instill a deep and lasting love of reading. We are involved and giving of ourselves that our children might become lifelong readers.

Everywhere I turn, I see children being given the tools they need, but not the heart. We bribe them to read (paying them so much per book for every book they read). We use reading as a punishment ("No more television. Go read in your room").

We want them to read for love. Read because it touches the depths of your soul. Books speak to your individuality. Come to know yourself and the world through the written word. It is rich and so very valuable. This is what we must attempt to convey to our youth. And the best way of doing it is by modeling. In fact, modeling is the only way.

Enough already! On with my list.

Artell, Mike *Petite Rouge: A Cajun Red Riding Hood*

This is, without question, my favorite read aloud for this age group. It might be in part due to my French Canadian heritage, but I think not. My wife, Vicki, loves it as much as I do and she is everything English. My friend and colleague Sally Bender gave this parody on Little Red Riding Hood to our Victoria, inscribed, "Victoria, this will touch your daddy's heart and soul." It has and is sure to touch yours. The illustrations are magnificent! However, the true pleasure in the book lies in the intriguing takeoff on Little Red Riding Hood and in the dialect: Cajun . . . that old, American, southern French. As you read it aloud, you will sound as if you are right out of a dangerous old swamp, deep in the heart of Louisiana. And yes, our Victoria loves it as much as we do.

> *Back in de swamp*
> *where dat Spanish moss grow,*
> *I heard me a story*
> *from long time ago.*

In a little ol' house
dat been built outta wood,
live a girl people call
Petite Rouge Riding Hood.

Becker, Helaine *Mama Likes to Mambo* ❦

This was Victoria's favorite book when she was three. There is room in every child's collection for a variety of styles of books. Helaine Becker's *Mama Likes to Mambo* is an example of my favorite genre to read to the very young. This collection of exciting, goofy poems will help you develop a reading style of your own. You'll just love mamboing your way through poem after poem in this wonderful Canadian picture book.

> A couple of years ago, I was speaking at a conference in Toronto. Vicki and Victoria were with me as it was past my five sleeps away from home limit. For a brief moment while touring the display area, we lost our girl. Within moments we recognized her laugh coming from a publisher's booth. We rounded the corner to find Victoria in deep conversation with Helaine Becker. Our angel had made a friend — an author no less. We thanked this warm, friendly woman while purchasing her book *Mama Likes to Mambo*. Helaine personalized it for Victoria. We took what had already become her favorite book up to our hotel room to discover that it was also our favorite.
>
> Educators, put on your thinking caps. What can you do to personalize books for the children in your school? An author visit is an obvious strategy, but there is so much more.
>
> My friend Don Robertson, principal of Earl Grey School in Calgary, purchases an original illustration from a children's book once a year if possible. These are mounted and displayed in the hallway of the school. Books at Earl Grey are a fun, living entity.

Boynton, Sandra *Barnyard Dance!*

Sandra Boynton is a prolific and gifted writer. Her books ooze rhythm and rhyme. I often find myself reading one of her books feeling frustrated that I did not write it myself. Of her numerous titles, *Barnyard Dance!* is my favorite. When you read this exciting poem about life on the farm, be sure that the room is clear. You will want to move your feet and clap your hands and dance to the rhythm of her Barnyard Dance!

Dodd, Lynley *Slinky Malinki*

Children of all ages love series (as do we adults). I discovered these books of fun, rhythmic poems featuring the charming cat Slinky Malinki while holidaying in Britain. It is huge on that island, so I wasn't surprised to come home and find it on many library shelves here in Canada. Robbie Burns once said that a poem isn't really a poem unless it has rhyme and rhythm. What a perfect way to introduce children to poetry through the books that they are coming to love! I find that reading stories written in rhythm and rhyme is delightful, and our Victoria insists on finishing most lines for me. Vicki, Victoria and I love this series as we do Dodd's equally attractive *Hairy Maclary*.

Elting, Mary and Michael Folsom *Q Is for Duck*

You cannot have too many books that focus on language development. And not all books are created equal. This little treasure is aimed at the higher end of this age group. It is a fun look at the alphabet. It is fun to read, challenging for young minds and certain to be a read-aloud success.

Kovalski, Maryann *Queen Nadine* ❦

This beautiful picture book about an unusual cow and the amazing discovery that she makes is sure to touch your hearts. Stephen Krashen suggests that television is not the enemy in getting our children reading. He believes that the lack of good books is the problem. If anything, it might be that some children do not have access to good books, but they are out there. Many are written, illustrated and published right here in Canada. They are worth seeking out.

Martin, Bill, Jr. *Brown Bear, Brown Bear, What Do You See?*

Bill Martin Jr. is an icon among childrens' writers. His books overflow our shelves. *Brown Bear, Brown Bear* is perhaps his best known and most successful. His use of repetition in this classic little tale epitomizes good writing. Our editor, Maggie, is going to have her work cut out limiting the number of times I recommend a Bill Martin book for early readers. He has been my mentor since 1990, when I had the pleasure of hearing him read *Ghost-Eye Tree*.

Mollel, Tololwa *Kitoto the Mighty* ❦

It is not necessary to hear this colorful tale read by the author himself, but what a thrill it was for me. I've read it to my own Victoria dozens of times, and each time I read it, I do a better reading than the time before. Mollel's voice will jump out at you and your child through each and every word. This old Jamaican tale, retold by a new Canadian writer, is sure to be a big-time favorite.

Musgrave, Susan *Dreams Are More Real Than Bathtubs* ❦

This is yet another marvelous picture book published by a Canadian publisher, written by a Canadian author and illustrated by the talented Canadian artist Marie-Louise Gay. This lovely tale is spun around a little girl who could be any of our children. Musgrave has captured the charm and humor of my daughter, Victoria. You will quickly identify her characters as being children somewhere close to you.

Nichol, Barbara *Trunks All Aboard: An Elephant ABC* ❦

Books that focus on counting, colors and the alphabet are a must for every collection of children's books. In *An Elephant ABC*, you will be charmed by a piece of Canadian folklore. The illustrations are by the great railroader William Van Horne. In this beautiful book you'll discover history, spectacular art and the alphabet presented in a most clever manner. Once you place this treasure on your own bookshelf, you will want to purchase it for friends and family. Think of this one as a coffee-table book for children.

Numeroff, Laura Joffe *If You Give a Mouse a Cookie*

Tens of thousands of teachers can't be wrong. I find few books in school and classroom libraries as consistently as I do *If You Give a Mouse a Cookie*. Teachers like it for many different reasons, not the least of which is that it makes an excellent model for children writing their own stories. You will enjoy the progression of natural thought patterns as well as the exciting illustrations. Kids love discovering exactly what happens if you give a mouse a cookie!

Rylant, Cynthia *Mr. Putter and Tabby Bake the Cake*

Children often ask me the name of my favorite author. Cynthia Rylant's name is always right on the tip of my tongue. She writes books that usually move me to tears. The Mr. Putter series is not one of those tear-filled reads, but it is a sweet and moving account of the life of an old man called Mr. Putter. This is the only book on this list that is not a picture book. Reading chapter books quickly becomes a source of pride in young children. Reading about Mr. Putter will offer them that feeling of pride!

Sendak, Maurice *Where the Wild Things Are*

An international best-selling classic! No collection can be without *Where the Wild Things Are*. When my four-year-old became frightened by some of the pictures in her Dr. Seuss books, I was certain that she'd not take to Sendak's voyage into the sleep world that features an entire group of horrific little creatures, but she loves them. This affection, which is common with many young children, might be due to the fact that the characters are seen everywhere, in many different forms. Sendak's Wild Things adorn the shelves of most libraries and book and toy stores. This book is a classic for every good reason.

Seuss, Dr. *The Cat in the Hat*

Dr. Seuss is arguably the most read and influential children's author of the twentieth century. His books are everywhere and have been read by almost everyone. It truly doesn't matter which of his books you choose to add to your collection first, over time you'll come to own several. *The Cat in the Hat* is our favorite.

Silverstein, Shel *The Giving Tree*

I carry this book with me wherever I go. It reminds me that a powerful message can be delivered through few words. This is a touching story of a boy who, from his youth through his old age, takes everything a beautiful tree has to offer. *The Giving Tree* explores the themes of giving and sharing. The illustrations are simple, but delightful. The text is concise and to the point. The message is one that all children should hear. This is an amazing little book!

Thompson, Richard *Then and Now* ✤

As has happened to us, you are sure to become a collector of the works of Richard Thompson once you've read any one of a number of this brilliant Canadian author's books. *Then and Now* moves you and your child through a series of life events that starts one way and finishes another. Through rhyme and rhythm, it encourages language acquisition in young children in addition to challenging their minds. Richard Thompson books will not disappoint.

Richard Thompson is a marvelous and affordable school presenter. While a principal in West Vancouver, I had Richard in to speak to our primary and intermediate students and discovered *Then and Now*. I also discovered that a big part of his focus is on sand stories. He awed my students for hours. I really shouldn't be so forceful in this as I missed much of their reaction. *I* was in awe. I later discovered that Richard's sand stories are available on-line. You can go to his site (www.drawandtell.com) and download one or more that you can use with your own children. His site is filled with creativity and excitement. There is more than Disney out there, and much of it is Canadian. Be sure to use the Internet to its fullest. It has many uses in promoting reading.

Wood, Audrey *King Bidgood's in the Bathtub*

This is one of the best-illustrated books that I own. It might be my all-time favorite. I'd buy *King Bidgood's in the Bathtub* a dozen times over, only for the illustrations. Couple the creative story of a king who refuses to get out of his bathtub with language that is rich in rhythm and you have a book that is sure to be a success with everyone. It simply must be in your library.

Part II: *Anne Letain*

When I looked over my final choices for this list, two themes jumped out at me.

The first was the young child exploring his own small world for the first time. Here there are books that explore what it's like to be getting ready for the world of school (colors, numbers and letters), as well as books that just plain celebrate the work of being a kid—going to sleep, choosing clothes to wear, getting in trouble, giving up a favorite comfort.

But there is also a secondary theme beyond the content of the books. In almost every book on this list, the illustrations are wholly integrated into the book and can almost stand on their own. No one style or medium is used, but as a whole they are remarkably rich—to be enjoyed over and over again!

I am reminded once again that there is no age limit to enjoying fabulous books.

Carle, Eric *The Very Hungry Caterpillar*

Recently reissued on its twenty-fifth birthday, *The Very Hungry Caterpillar* is now a "real" classic in children's literature. As the very hungry caterpillar munches his way to his ultimate destiny as a beautiful butterfly, parent and child alike will enjoy Carle's trademark collage illustrations and spiffy design.

Johnson, Crockett *Harold and the Purple Crayon*

Enchanting children since 1955, Harold and his purple crayon go on a journey of imagination that sees Harold conducting a terrific adventure while keeping his wits about him—creating a purple boat when he finds himself in deep water or drawing a purple pie when he's famished. For Harold, anything is possible, and you can follow his destiny in a number of sequels. Compelling in its simplicity. Children love to create their own purple drawings.

Krauss, Ruth *A Hole Is to Dig: A First Book of First Definitions*

This is a unique book of definitions, which is difficult to describe but totally captivating on one level for adults and on another for children. It's an overlooked classic bit of fun as simple definitions are turned topsy-turvy ("A hole is to dig"). The simple illustrations are early Maurice Sendak and integrate well with the concept of the book. Childhood in a nutshell.

Martin, Bill, Jr., and John Archambault
Chicka Chicka Boom Boom

Likely one of the best alphabet books ever conceived, *Chicka Chicka Boom Boom* resonates with an irresistible rhythm that presents children with many opportunities to join in. It just hums along. Lois Ehlert's illustrations are a brilliant and colorful complement to the text and invite easy identification of lowercase letters. Easily accessed in many formats.

Murphy, Jill *The Last Noo-Noo*

This is a really witty book about the need for Marlon the Monster to give up his pacifier (aka noo-noo). Marlon is feeling a lot of pressure from the grown-ups in his life to give up his best friend. However, he comes up with a truly original solution to soften the pain. The pictures have vintage Murphy charm as well.

> When I start finding a certain book "hidden" in the library, I know I have a winning title going for me. One of my current top hidden books is *The Last Noo-Noo* by Jill Murphy. Here's how it works: You come in to the library and notice that the book is available. You haven't got time to get it for yourself, but you don't want anyone else to have it either. So you put it somewhere (among other books, of course) where you can retrieve it later and claim your prize when your class comes down to the library. The other way to get the book is to stalk the kid who has it and take it before it is officially returned.

Pace, David *Shouting Sharon: A Riotous Counting Rhyme*

Shouting Sharon is an original counting book that features an anticipatory set that is suspenseful and provides lots of outright fun for children as they guess what Sharon will shout out next. The ending is entirely unexpected. As an added bonus, the text employs some catchy alliteration. Illustrations are comic and colorful.

Rosen, Michael *We're Going on a Bear Hunt*

Based on the old campfire activity, *We're Going on a Bear Hunt* is way more than a story — it's a rhythmic chant that gains momentum as it reaches its ultimate finale (the bear!). Kids just love making all the sounds (mud squishing, grass swooshing, etc.), and they'll beg for it to be read over and over again. Lots of plain old silliness along with excellent illustrations from Helen Oxenbury.

Shannon, David *No, David!*

Loosely autobiographical, *No, David!* is an affectionate remembrance by David Shannon of his early years. Every parent and child will be able to identify with David's misdemeanors, but will also be able to affirm the lovely ending. The illustrations are bold, breezy and somewhat daring as far as kids are concerned. *No, David!* is part of a trilogy, which includes *David Goes to School* and *David Gets in Trouble*.

No, David! is worn out from all the love and attention it receives from kindergarten. I was unable to get a hardcover version, and the paperback is worn out even though it's been on the shelf less than six months. I find the kids just giggling over two particular pages — the one where David is picking his nose, and the one where he's roaring down the street au naturel. I guess I'm going to have to find a way to get a new hardcover copy before the current copy totally dies!

Tolhurst, Marilyn
Somebody and the Three Blairs

This is a lovely version of an old favorite with some added twists. It features "Somebody" as the bear and the "Blairs" as people. Its gentle flavor really appeals to kindergarten-aged children, and they beg to hear it again and again. They identify with Baby Blair and his penchant for mischief.

Vaage, Carol *Bibi and the Bull* ❦

This is a terrific little book for the preschool crowd about Bibi's visit to her grandfather's farm. Bibi is reminded about the many dangers around the farm, but she manages to find trouble in spite of the warnings. How Bibi manages to get out of trouble is the real charm of the book, along with Georgia Graham's original artwork. The bull and the cows are amazing. Graham has a well-earned reputation as the cow artist.

Waddell, Martin *Can't You Sleep, Little Bear?*

This is the quintessential bedtime book for parents. As Little Bear grapples with his fear of the dark, Big Bear patiently provides larger and larger lanterns to dispel the shadows. At last, Little Bear drifts off to sleep, secure and safe in Big Bear's arms. The writing is gentle and easy and Barbara Firth's illustrations are visually relaxing.

Waddell, Martin *The Pig in the Pond*

While watching the ducks splash in the pond on a very hot summer's day, the pig becomes hotter and hotter and more and more frustrated. The sweltering pig dives in with uproarious consequences. This is the perfect rip-roaring read aloud for those sticky summer afternoons. A total hoot!

Walsh, Ellen Stoll *Mouse Count*

Dramatic collages illustrate the story of heroic mice who outwit cats and snakes and learn to count along the way. Some parents may object to the snake regarding the mice as "warm and tasty," but others might see it as an opportunity to explain the concept of predator and prey. Purchase *Mouse Count* along with *Mouse Paint* for an exceptional set of concept books for preschoolers.

Wattenberg, Jane *Henny-Penny*

This is one very noisy version of Henny-Penny — the chicken with sky anxiety. It is awash in rhyme, repetition and fun. Wattenberg employs a kind of photographic collage to illustrate her vision of the story. The book has great visual appeal and is replete with sly wit, which will be attractive to the adult sharing this book with a young child.

Part III: *Sally Bender*

This is an age group that is so much fun when you want to share books. They are the perfect audience if you are prepared to have a hilarious time while you read. They want to hear all your funny voices and delight in acting out the events of the story. The more fun you have with them, the more memorable the book and the more they want to hear it again.

Almost every book that I have chosen for my list allows the reader to take the lead and to encourage the listener to become part of the conversation that accompanies the reading. The language is enlightening and the art is detailed and bold. Your task is set and you are on your way to great fun and precious time spent with the children you love.

Alborough, Jez *Duck in the Truck*

Jez Alborough has written some of my favorite books for this age group. Here's why . . .

When Duck gets his truck stuck in the muck, he counts on good friends to help him out. First, Frog tries to push, but it is a no go. When Sheep drives up in his Jeep, he yells at Duck and his stuck truck to get out of the way. Sheep, Frog and Duck cannot get it unstuck. Goat, floating by in his boat, proves to be the catalyst needed to move the truck. As Duck happily heads for home, he forgets all about his three friends . . . still stuck in the muck!

Humor, terrific rhythmic language and friends helping friends make this yarn memorable and often requested at story time.

Bang, Molly *When Sophie Gets Angry — Really, Really Angry . . .*

Kids can tell by looking at the cover of this book that trouble is brewing. They note the hot colors and Sophie's tense face. Sisters are not always best at taking turns when it comes to their toys, and Sophie explodes when she doesn't get her way. In her anger, she slams out of the house. Soon, she is crying. As she walks farther into the surrounding woods, she begins to notice all the things that she loves . . . the birds, the ocean breeze, the old beech tree. Her world brings comfort. Arriving back home, Sophie is no longer angry and she is able to join a family activity.

We could all take a lesson from Sophie in managing our anger and stress. This book invites discussion, and Molly Bang has created glorious art to set the mood.

Brown, Ken *Mucky Pup*

Just another puppy to love! The farmer's wife does not appreciate the chaos that one exuberant pup can create, so he is booted outdoors. Still wanting to play, he seeks a companion. But the haughty animals of the farmyard refuse his invitations. Then he meets an equally mucky pig, and the games begin! An inadvertent splash into the pond brings an end to the play and to Mucky Pup's eventful day. In the final illustration, he is resting up for another day of fun and frolic with his new friend.

The repetitive language and the haughty responses of the farm animals provide humor mixed with sadness as Mucky Pup searches for a like-minded friend.

Read it again, Dad!

Dodds, Dayle Ann *Sing, Sophie!*

One of my favorite read-aloud stories, despite the fact that I make a fool of myself each time I read it. This is a book that begs to be read again and again. Sophie has a voice that only a mother could love, but she loves to sing and she does so with enthusiasm. No one appreciates her talent and they are always sending her somewhere else to do her caterwaulin'. Poor Sophie! But when a thunderstorm wakes her baby brother, only Sophie can sing him back to sleep.

You need no musical ability to sing Sophie's songs, just a sense of humor and a lack of decorum.

Our school counselor's office is in a corner of the library. Unless she closes her door, she often falls victim to the stories I share with the kids on a daily basis. My singing is bearable until I share *Sing, Sophie!* It begs the reader to ham it up and that is just what I do whenever I read it.

One morning, at my loudest and corniest, I turned to find that everyone attending a team meeting in the counselor's office was standing in the library, listening to the story. They could not help but be drawn to the laughter and loudness of the telling. They were worried that some kind of mischief was being wrought. Besides that, they were getting nothing done while I sang Sophie's songs with all the mayhem I could muster.

Ehlert, Lois *Hands*

Lois Ehlert's bold and beautiful color collages illustrate concept books that beg to be shared.

In *Hands*, Lois gives us a glimpse into the events that led to her life's work. Her father, a carpenter; her mother, a designer; and Lois, a combination of the two, are the inspiration for *Hands*, designed to look like a pair of gloves. We discover the tools of each one's trade and learn how the parents inspired Lois to try her hand at whatever interested her. Lois promises to keep working at her table and developing her art, knowing that when she grows up she will join hands with her mom and dad.

Emberley, Ed *Go Away, Big Green Monster!*

When our kids were little, we read *Goodnight Moon* and *Green Eggs and Ham* until we could say them in our sleep. To this day, I can recite most of the words. Some books inspire a nonstop demand for more.

Such is the case with this monster book in my kindergarten class and everywhere else I read it. The art is inspired. The book allows young children to invite a scary monster into their realm and then rid themselves of it in a moment. My kids do not call it an "old" favorite; they call it an "always" favorite. Young children can soon read it alone, and the three copies that we have in our class are taken home daily in our bedtime book bags. A must read for your family!

I am often asked to do workshops with adults about children's literature. The topic may vary, but I always share one or more of the books that I bring with my audience. At a professional development session where I was talking about great read alouds, I began with *Go Away, Big Green Monster!* The audience, as usual, was attentive and caught up in the reading. As I roared the last line, two audience members called out, "Oh! Please read it again!" Now that is a real test of the impact that picture books can have . . . for all ages.

Feiffer, Jules *Bark, George*

George's mother is patient as she encourages George to learn to talk; she uses her most persuasive voice and sets the tone for his learning. But George finds it difficult to bark. It takes a trip to the vet and a lot of hilarity to get to the bottom of the problem. Children laugh uproariously as they discover the pattern to the story. The surprise ending has them rolling in the aisles and begging for another telling. The characters are appealing and the action predictable. This is a must have.

Fleming, Denise *Alphabet Under Construction*

Our school library has more than one hundred alphabet books. Our staff are constantly amazed that artists are able to come up with groundbreaking ideas to help children learn about the twenty-six letters that determine our language. In *Alphabet Under Construction*, Denise Fleming sets Mouse (an old friend) the task of using the tools of his trade to construct an alphabet. With buttons, nails, chisels, erasers, glue, pulleys and even tiles, the letters emerge in the bold, familiar colors of Fleming's pulp paintings. The verbs are often new and descriptive. This book will add flavor to the construction vocabulary of any aspiring carpenter.

Fleming, Denise *Time to Sleep*

As summer bids its farewell and fall begins, the forest inhabitants note the changes that are taking place around them. Bear is the first to notice the smell of winter in the air. She knows she must find a cave for hibernation, but first she must prepare her friend, Snail. Snail has noticed the frost on the grass and is determined to warn Skunk. And so it goes. Each animal delivers the news to a friend. Finally, Ladybug hears and knows she must tell Bear. At last, all tucked in for the winter, the only thing left is to wish each other "Good night!" They do so . . . endlessly.

Fox, Mem *Tough Boris*

Mem Fox says that it is so easy to get picture books wrong and so hard to get them right. She finds it a daunting task to give children what they deserve: the very best. She chooses each word carefully and rewrites over and over again.

Seventy words tell the story in *Tough Boris*; each word is chosen to have the perfect impact on the young reader. Boris has few redeeming qualities, but when his parrot dies he shows the kindness and compassion of all human beings when faced with the death of a loved one.

This is a book to be savored and discussed.

Gammell, Stephen
Once Upon MacDonald's Farm

Old MacDonald's Farm is not what we expect. How can we sing about a farm with no animals? And when Old MacDonald sets out to buy some, his choices are unconventional, to say the least. The animals tire of the drudgery of farm work and leave in the dead of night. Once again, Old MacDonald has nothing. As the story unfolds, we realize what an inept farmer MacDonald really is.

I have been reading this wonderful book to classes for years, and I never tire of it. The art is filled with unspoken details and Gammell's irreverent humor. The final illustration is inspiring!

Stinson, Kathy *Red Is Best*

In our family, the best color is purple. Purple goes with everything and inspires feelings of power and happiness. Kathy Stinson introduces us to a wee girl who has much to say about the color red. Twenty-five years after she first appeared in print, Kelly's mom still does not understand the importance of red!

Moms never understand about red. They don't understand that red stockings are best with a blue and white dress. They don't understand that you can't be Red Riding Hood in a blue winter jacket, even if it is cold outside. And they don't understand that red mittens with holes are much better than warm brown woolen mittens. Red mittens make better snowballs. Red pajamas scare away the monsters at night. Juice tastes better in a red cup. When will mothers learn? Red is best . . . and that is all there is to it. *Red Is Best* is the perfect lap book for sharing between a mom and a little girl. As appealing as ever.

Red paint puts singing in my head.

Wells, Rosemary *Noisy Nora*

Rosemary Wells captures perfectly the thoughts and feelings of the young as they struggle with the agonies of growing up.

Nora notices everything about her family, especially that no one is paying any attention to her. Being Nora, she has some ideas about how to attract an audience. First, she bangs a window and slams a door, bringing brief negative attention before everyone goes back to work. Nora has to wait, but waiting is not her game. Still desperate for attention, she leaves. The family searches everywhere. Nora waits until they are distraught and stages a resounding return. Everyone is happy.

Wood, Audrey *The Napping House*

Cumulative stories are a great way to introduce young readers to the pleasure of repetitive text and to show them how a story grows and becomes new by adding more words.

We come to the napping house in a rainstorm. Dull skies and streaks of rain fill the page as we enter the napping house to find everyone asleep. On the cozy bed lies a snoring granny. As the action unfolds, she is joined by a dreaming child, a dozing dog, a snoozing cat and a slumbering mouse. When a wakeful flea is added to the mix, mayhem follows.

The exuberance of the artwork and the changing mood of the story will have your audience glued to this book. The colors move from the muted blues and grays of a rainy day to the warmth of yellow sunshine as the entire house is awakened.

Part IV: *Lucie Poulin-Mackey*

Now we can really start having fun with books and children! The books in this list appeal to your child's sense of imagination, which is starting to develop. Children are sponges at this age and retain enormous quantities of information. They repeat songs and stories from their favorite shows. They sing the same tunes forever and never get bored of hearing the same story over and over again. If French is not the child's mother tongue, this is a great age to introduce a second language. I've included stories to nurture the imagination and entice play. I've also included books that deal with real-life issues such as day care and preschool. Books are not only interesting at this age, but also become fun. I hope that this list will provide hours of entertainment for all.

Barclay, Jane *Quel froid de canard !*
French text by Cécile Gagnon

You will need a blanket to read this book. It is a cold, cold morning. How cold is it? So cold that your teeth chatter and you have to stay under the covers. Jack Frost paints the windows. The cars won't start. Sound familiar? This book reminded me of my childhood in northern Ontario and what could warm us up . . . hot chocolate, warm porridge and a good fire in the fireplace. A feel-good book for all.

Blegvad, Erik *La véritable histoire des trois petits cochons*
French text by Élisée Escande

We all know the story of the three little pigs, but in this version the wolf has grown a little wiser by the time he gets to the last little pig. Loving a challenge, the pig agrees to meet the wolf in the cabbage patch to see who can pick the most cabbage. The little pig cleverly arrives an hour ahead of time and is safe back in his house by the appointed meeting hour. The wolf has been duped once again. The story continues in the same fashion until the wolf grows annoyed and tries to enter the house by the chimney. You guessed it . . . that's the end for him. A cute twist to this classic tale that will please all readers.

Bourgeois, Paulette *Benjamin va à la maternelle*
French text by Lucie Duchesne ❀

Benjamin is a little nervous on his first day of school, all the way from the bus ride to walking through the classroom door. In the end, Benjamin overcomes his fears, makes friends and enjoys school. These are the toddler versions of the well-loved Franklin series. This cute turtle has created a reading frenzy at all levels. A television series, stuffed animals and games accompany him. Benjamin is endearing to all. My office is full of Benjamin dolls and books. This is a favorite.

Faulkner, Keith *L'ours qui ne pouvait pas dormir*
French text by Jacob d'Angelo

"RÂÂÂON PSCHIIIII!!!!!!!" What could that noise be? It's enough to wake up Little Bear. He's scared. Could it be a bear, a lion or an elephant? Should he call his dad? "Papa," says Little Bear very quietly. Papa doesn't answer. "Papa," says Little Bear, a little more loudly this time. Still no answer. Little Bear musters up his courage to go find his dad because only Dad can save him from this monster. In his parents' room, the secret of the noise is revealed. A wonderful read-aloud book. The pop-up images are vivid and nurturing to the imagination. The conclusion reveals what may be close to home. A big book with big pictures. A great bedtime story.

Car seul son papa peut le protéger du terrible monstre.

Ferron, Nicole (Translator) *Bambou va à la garderie*

"Bambou, you are going to day care." These are scary words for a young child. Day care means away from Mom and Dad. In this story, Bambou, a chimp, learns that day care can be fun. Day care includes play time, story time and snack time. With bold letters and few words, the author demystifies day care. This is a great book to help your child learn what to expect, thus easing his or her transition from home to day care. Other Bambou adventures explore different themes such as honesty, fire, drawing on walls and getting lost.

Galbert, Elizabeth *Le voyage d'Amédée*

Discover the colors of the rainbow through this beautiful book. Amédée, the bear, travels the world in search of friends of different species. She discovers animals, names of things and so much more. Written in simple, easy text, the story will help young readers discover new words and build their vocabulary. The book incorporates shiny paper into different animals and objects.

Hamel, Judith *Modo et la lune* ✤

The moon has been an object of fascination for thousands of years. Not long ago, we sent a man to the moon. It stands to reason that a bear would share our fascination. One night at bedtime, Modo discovers a ray of light in his room. As he clears the frost from his window with his warm breath, he notices the moon and is worried that she might be cold. Discover the tender relationship that evolves between Modo and the moon. Another good bedtime story.

La lune, émue par la tendresse de l'ourson,
le fait monter sur son rayon de lumière.

Jolin, Dominique *Attends une minute!* 🍁

To Camilien, waiting a minute when he is thirsty is as bad as having to wait for days. It's like crossing the desert in a sandstorm or being transformed into a mummy. Camilien helps us to realize just what we are asking of children when time and time again we say to them, "Wait a minute." Dominique Jolin's use of color and texture takes the reader into a world of discovery. The reader is swept through a series of locations, from a dry, ant-infested desert to a sky filled with flying dragons to the churning waters of the lobster-filled ocean. And all in just one minute! The simple text makes this book a good read aloud any time, including bedtime.

Keats, Ezra Jack *Jour de neige*

French text by Catherine Bonhomme

Ah!! The magic of fresh snow. Who hasn't been mesmerized by it? Peter wakes up one morning to see snow for the very first time. With few words per page, the author evokes the wonder of that first discovery of snow. Follow Peter as he discovers the endless activities related to this extraordinary white fluffy powder. He slides; he makes a snowman; he makes snow angels. A good read on a snowy day. The English version of this story won the Caldecott Medal.

Klinting, Lars *Le petit menuisier*

Today busy Beaver has decided that he will dabble in a little carpentry. With his plan in hand, Beaver can now begin to build something. What will it be? From the measuring to the final product, the reader is involved in every step of the construction while learning the names of the tools.

The perfect book for the young carpenter-to-be. My son loves this book so much that Santa had to bring tools for his stocking. There have been no loose screws in our house since Christmas.

Masurel, Claire *Dix chiens dans la vitrine*

There are ten dogs in the pet shop window. Which dog will be bought by the passerby? Will the dalmation be bought by the fireman or the jogger? A cute story to help the child count from ten to one, it is written in rhymes encouraging predictions. In the end the dogs are gone. What kind of animals will go in the window next? This is a good book to fire up the imagination.

Menola, Caroline *N'aie pas peur Nic !* 🍁

Olivier has a best friend. His name is Nic. Nic has saved people from a burning building; he has caught robbers; he can climb trees. Did I mention that Nic is a bear? Olivier and Nic do everything together. One day Nic invites Olivier for a sleepover. As strong as he is, Nic is afraid of only one thing: the dark. It is Olivier's turn to be the hero. An endearing story of friendship that will be enjoyed by all.

> *Heureusement, les gros oursons ont le poil doux et long*
> *et un bedon bien chaud pour rassurer les petits garçons.*

In our household we read a lot, all genres. Our youngest is fascinated by anything that moves, that has a motor and that makes noise. His choice of books, then, is not surprising: Tonka books, the *Auto Trader* and such. What luck it was when we discovered a book with his name, Olivier, in it. *N'aie pas peur Nic !* is a new favorite. He is proud to bring this book to school and show his friends that he is its star!

Munsch, Robert *Je t'aimerai toujours* 🍁
French text by Robert Paquin

Take out your tissues. If this book is not in your child's library, it should at least be in yours. To this day my youngest son chooses this book for me to read to him at bedtime if he's had a particularly interesting day as far as personal discipline is concerned. (Know what I mean?) This is more a mom book than a kid book, but both my sons love it because I sing them their favorite song at the page we like to call the Elvis page. (That's another story.) They also like the bathroom scene because it reminds them of their own lives. Another day I will tell you (and Robert Munsch himself) about the egg incident, but I'm still not over it. There must be a book there.

This is a feel-great book that will bring you closer to your child.

Richards, Nancy W. *Pas de dodo sans doudou*

French text by Christiane Duchesne

Meet Antoine (Farmer Joe) in his latest adventure, baby-sitting for the first time. Poor Antoine is left by himself with Marie-Jeanne. Marie-Jeanne must have a nap in the afternoon and will not sleep without her blankie. Antoine takes his charge exploring around the farm, and when naptime comes, the blanket is nowhere to be found. This book was a finalist for the Communication-Jeunesse Award.

Vaillancourt, Danielle *Trop c'est trop!* ❦

"I want a dog!!!!" but Mom wants anything but. Extreme measures are called for: No dog, no kisses. As luck would have it, Mom can't live without kisses. So off to the pet store we go. Néva chooses the funniest, loudest dog she can. He has big ears, moves too much and is certain to wreak havoc in the household. He is perfect! "Sit Max . . . but not on the hamster!" "Eat Max . . . but not Mom's supper!" Will Max ever learn? Then Mom declares that enough is enough. Is Max headed for the shelter?

Chapter Three

Six- to Eight-Year-Olds

Part 1: *David Bouchard*

Children at this age often start to seek out their own reading independence. I've said often and not always. Do not rush your child. Nothing, anywhere, dictates that children should be ready to read independently at the age of five or six, or eight, for that matter. Reading readiness cannot and should not be rushed. Be wary of programs that push children beyond their natural abilities. We are in the midst of a terrible trend in North America to push our children to read before they are ready. Whether they are ready or not, we introduce all children to exactly the same material, material that we deem appropriate. We often teach them to read for every wrong reason. We expect them to understand and to be able to respond to our questioning. Then we test them. And finally, to what should be our eternal shame, we label many of our children.

Sadly, many of our new reading initiatives are actually setbacks and deterrents as we seek to turn our children into lifelong readers. A plethora of initiatives push and probe children well beyond their limits. When you consider using one of these, you risk robbing your children of any and all pleasure and value that reading might otherwise have brought them.

For example, in 1999, a program was initiated in the U.S. called Start Early — Finish Strong. The purpose was to get children reading early. The theory is that children should learn to read at the earliest of ages so that they might get to some specific destination in life — and the faster they get there, the better. By learning to read early, children should do better on exams and thus succeed in school. Sadly, this is not happening. Many children are not ready to read at the specified times, and those who are ready are being given the skills that will allow them to read, but not the heart. We are teaching them to read for the wrong reasons. They do not grow up reading for pleasure. They can read, but they are choosing not to read. Mark Twain said, "Those who can but who choose not to read have no advantage over those who cannot read." What gift are we giving our children?

Recently, star NBA basketball players have been appearing on television with a message for kids. They are telling children that they have become successful basketball players by reading. Our kids don't buy that. They know how these athletes found success and they don't believe them to be avid readers. Children do not believe that Shaq O'Neil owes his success to his having read *Charlotte's Web*. Most children believe that reading is not a big part of the lives of top athletes. And they are right. The NBA's program is called Read to Achieve. That is not the message we want to teach our children.

We should not be selling reading as a tool or a road to get anywhere. It should and must be presented for what it is . . . a personal experience that allows the reader to access people and places, all within the confines of one's own mind and imagination.

Give your children and your students the room and the time to grow. Let them enjoy picture books as long as they like. Allow them to decide when to start reading chapter books. Never stop reading to them. And above all, choose books that appeal to you as well as to your children.

Baum, L. Frank *The Wonderful Wizard of Oz*

I could never plan a book list without *The Wonderful Wizard of Oz*. My favorite version of this timeless classic of Dorothy traveling to and through Oz with the three sad souls all children learn to love is the one illustrated by Charles Santore. You'll keep it forever.

Carrier, Roch *The Hockey Sweater* ❧

English text by Sheila Fischman

No other children's book better captures the competition between English and French Canadians than *The Hockey Sweater* does. The story of betrayal and disappointment that a young Quebecois boy feels when he receives a Toronto Maple Leafs sweater rather than a Montreal Canadiens sweater has become a children's classic. All Canadians should own this book.

Demers, Dominique *Old Thomas and the Little Fairy* ❦
English text by Sheila Fischman

The illustrations in this book about an old man who stumbles across and falls in love with a lovely fairy are stunning. The story is one of magic and touching love. This is not your normal child, but one of minute stature and strength, totally dependent on an old, unhappy fisherman. All this with Stéphane Poulin's spectacular illustrations. Another sure winner.

de Vries, Maggie *Chance and the Butterfly* ❦

Most of my recommended books on this list are picture books. From time to time, I find a book that is gentle and captivating—one that shares an important message. Children want and deserve respect. Don't just talk, say something. My friend and colleague Maggie de Vries does this in *Chance and the Butterfly*. This is a gentle and sensitive portrayal of a young boy finding strength, confidence and friends through a school science program. It's a book that you and your children are sure to enjoy.

Herriot, James *The Market Square Dog*

Although James Herriot's tales are set in a particular and well-drawn time and place, to me they feel timeless and without geographical boundaries. His tales of everyday experiences in the life of a vet on the Yorkshire Dales speak to the most gentle part of what our world can be. I find this book and this series calming, energizing and fulfilling. Victoria likes them as much as we do. The illustrations fit in perfectly.

Holden, Robert *The Pied Piper of Hamelin*

I love the romance of fairy tales, legends and stories of old. Many come from cultures other than and older than our own. I've always been fascinated by Cervantes' *Don Quixote*. And I've always loved the German legend of the Pied Piper. This version, incredibly well illustrated, is written in wonderful rhythm . . . with a touch of rhyme . . . just to make it perfect.

Jones, Terry *Fairy Tales*

Terry Jones is better known for his role in Monty Python movies than for his writing. However, I can assure you that everything nonsensical you'd hope to find in his movies is sure to be found in his books. This is a collection of short, funny, off-the-wall tales. They might not appeal to all children, but they sure do to me . . . AND to most other little boys.

Park, Barbara *Junie B. Jones and the Stupid Smelly Bus*

You can't be the parent/custodian or educator of a child in this age group and not know that the B in Junie B. Jones stands for Beatrice. This is a series that touches on many of life's situations, and each book is better than the one before! Junie B. is the most charming little girl you will ever meet, the best of Pollyanna and Matilda combined. Barbara Park is a gifted writer who opens the door to literacy in our homes and schools. Add the entire series to your collection. You'll have hours of fun reading them with your children. And as an added bonus, you'll be given umpteen opportunities to do what literacy is meant to allow you to do — or: come to share, with your children, your values, priorities and inner selves.

A few years ago as I was walking past the bedroom of my fourteen-year-old stepdaughter, I heard deep, strangled laughter. I tapped on the door and found Ashleigh and her girlfriend finishing off one of my Junie B. Jones books. They loved Junie B. as you are guaranteed to love her. This series is the ultimate in read alouds — guaranteed hits with all ages.

Riley, Wilma *Pies* ❦

Some children pick up and read anything and everything. Some need more of a hook. *Pies* is for those who need something different — something special. This clever book deals with cultural diversity. It addresses our need to be patient, understanding and compassionate. It is illustrated by Sheldon Cohen, who also illustrated Carrier's *Hockey Sweater*. Read this book to yourself before you share it. In it, a woman feeds her neighbor and archenemy cow-dung pie. Only during the feeding does she come to realize how alike she is to her neighbor. That revelation gives her only one option as she tries to right the wrong, and that's to eat a piece herself!

This is a book for reluctant and weak readers — a book that will capture and hold the interest of any reader, no matter how hard a sell he might be. I've read it to hundreds of children and it has yet to fail me. *Pies* is gross. Have you ever walked along a sidewalk realizing that there was a foul odor in the air that seemed to be following you? After a while you lift your foot to discover that you have dog excrement on the sole of your shoe. Your face curls into an expression of disgust. This is the look you will see on the faces of your children and students as you read *Pies* to them. Watch and listen. You will soon hear, "Oh GROSSSSSS!!! Read it again!"

Rowling, J.K. *Harry Potter and the Philosopher's Stone*
(*Sorcerer's Stone* in the U.S.)

Children deserve to read the Harry Potter series or to have it read to them. No one will deny the impact this series has had on the reading habits of today's youth. Rarely has a book, and then a series, had the influence that Harry Potter has had. I cannot imagine a parent or an educator anywhere making a reasonable argument for not having read the books themselves. There is none. Nor can I imagine anyone trying to argue that a child should be deprived of knowing Harry Potter. It would be terrible if the entire class were talking about a character or a scene from the book and one child was out of the loop. We all owe Harry Potter to our children. This is the time to start!

Van Allsburg, Chris *Jumanji*

I've recommended *Jumanji* as a Chris Van Allsburg book for your collection, but I could have chosen many of his others. *Jumanji* is an exciting story in which unsuspecting children enter a world of wild animals and eccentric hunters through a strange game that they discover quite by chance. Van Allsburg's work is collected the world over. His *Polar Express* is a Christmas must read, but he has many other treasures. *Jumanji* is one of my favorites. It has been made it into a superb movie featuring almost everyone's favorite, Robin Williams.

Peter took his turn. Thank heavens, he landed on a blank space. He rolled again. "Monsoon season

*begins, lose one turn." Little raindrops began to fall in
the living room. Then a roll of thunder shook the
walls and scared the monkeys out of the kitchen. The
rain began to fall in buckets as Judy took the dice.*

White, E.B. *Charlotte's Web*

I know that I've used the word favorite before, but forget all that. THIS is my all-time favorite children's book. It is the story of a sensitive, loving little pig named Wilbur whose life is saved first by a little girl and then by a most amazing spider named Charlotte. I've read it dozens of times and have never finished it without having to draw on a handful of tissues. It is that touching. Nor have I ever heard anything but praise for E.B. White's classic. For a real treat, pick up the CD or the cassette of E.B. White reading it himself.

Wilde, Oscar *The Fairy Tales of Oscar Wilde*

Oscar Wilde's tales are all winners, but there are two standouts. "The Happy Prince" is a sweet, comforting story of a statue that in life was a happy little prince; however, as a statue he is saddened and eventually broken by the poverty and suffering he witnesses in his city. And "The Selfish Giant," WONDERFUL! This touching classic is my favorite fairy tale ever.

Part II: *Anne Letain*

This list is about FUN! And maybe some more FUN! I have probably shared many of these titles a "dillion" times, in the language of my younger students. Each time I read one of these books I reflect on my good fortune. It's not often that you get to be a kid again and do something just for joy. These titles just roar off the shelf to be reread and savored and shared at home with parents, grandparents and siblings. I'm amazed at the sustained demand for them, and I often find myself purchasing additional copies and replacing those that have been "loved" to death and staples. There's something really irresistible here.

The ante on fairy tales has been upped, too. The fairy-tale titles here are not only creative and funny; they also presume a familiarity with the original versions. I realize that by the time I share these particular stories, I've done the spadework about fairy-tale characters and typical plot work. Although these books can stand on their own merits, they are even better when children know the original versions.

Allard, Harry *Miss Nelson Is Missing*

Primary-aged kids never tire of the fabulous Miss Nelson and her alter ego, Viola Swamp (aka "The Swamp"). When the kids in room 207 of Horace B. Smedley School are misbehaving, their teacher, Miss Nelson, takes things in hand and brings in the meanest substitute in the whole world. Or does she? Illustrator James Marshall used his own second-grade teacher as his inspiration for "The Swamp," and she has become a classic character in children's literature. Equally good are the sequels *Miss Nelson Is Back* and *Miss Nelson Has a Field Day*.

A teacher-librarian colleague's husband owns a silk-screening company, and I made a deal with her a few years ago. If I could get the appropriate wig, her husband would make us "The Swamp" hooded sweatshirt featured in *Miss Nelson Has a Field Day*, which says in bold white lettering "COACH, AND DON'T YOU FORGET IT!" So once a year, two teachers in southern Alberta get to act out their fantasy of being the meanest teacher in the universe. The kids love to go along for the ride. Besides, it's the only way I'll ever get to be a brunette in a ball cap!

Browne, Anthony *Piggybook*

Illustrator extraordinaire Anthony Browne has created a visual pièce de résistance in *Piggybook*. When Mrs. Piggott informs her husband and children that they have become slovenly pigs, she leaves the boys and their dad to their own devices. Everything in the Piggott world becomes porcine. You can read this book over and over again and still find pigs lurking in the strangest places. Although more famous for his simian (ape) creations, Browne's pigs are simply spectacular here. The ending is a triumph for budding feminists everywhere.

Brownridge, William Roy *The Moccasin Goalie* ❈

Loosely based on a childhood memory of the author, *The Moccasin Goalie* is the story of Danny, who earns a cherished place on the Wolves hockey team despite his crippled leg and his inability to wear skates. This is an essential prairie hockey story. Only the most jaded could resist being swept along by both the story and the mood of the long-gone outdoor community rink. Brownridge's paintings, particularly the double spreads, are dazzling and almost mesmerizing in their power to capture the low winter sun reflecting off the unending snowscape. Two sequels: *The Final Game* and *Victory at Paradise Hill*.

Emberley, Rebecca *Three Cool Kids*

As one of the Emberley clan of writers and illustrators, Rebecca Emberley has displayed her family's artistic and literary talents in this brilliant re-telling of "The Three Billy Goats Gruff." Constructed of paper collage in a wide variety of colors and textures and then photographed, the whole book is a visual treat. Emberley has chosen to tell this version in an urban ghetto setting featuring "Big," "Middle" and "Little" as the billy goats along with a really fearsome sewer rat as the ogre. The text is melodic and wonderful to read aloud.

Gilman, Phoebe *Something from Nothing* ❈

The late Phoebe Gilman's retelling of an old Jewish folktale is nothing short of wonderful. A young boy will not give up his old and tattered jacket and informs his mother that his grandfather will fix it. Grandfather (a tailor) changes the jacket into a vest, which in turn becomes tired and tattered. The boy goes back to his grandfather for help again and again, and in the end the grandfather is unable to create something from nothing. Gilman's illustrations are warm and generous, and she provides a second wordless story (à la Jan Brett) at the bottom of each page.

Something from Nothing is Senator Joyce Fairbairn's showcase piece for her literacy activities across the country. She has had a seamstress make from wonderful moon and star fabric all the items that Grandfather creates from Joseph's coat in the story. When she reads the story, she recruits a willing volunteer to wear the jacket. The poor child is so surprised and startled when Senator Fairbairn rips the sleeves off to create the vest! However, the children are soon right into the spirit of the story and are begging to be the one who wears the jacket. Senator Fairbairn also reads from the Braille version of the book and explains to the children how a blind parent would read the book to their child, or a blind child to the parent. The kids are fascinated by the reading performance and also by the chance to touch and examine the Braille version.

Henkes, Kevin *Lilly's Purple Plastic Purse*

No one does childhood defiance better than Kevin Henkes, and Lilly is one of his finest creations. Modeled and named after his own niece, Lilly receives a purple plastic purse, which she adores and insists on taking to school. When she cannot refrain from playing with it during class time, her favorite teacher temporarily removes it from her. Lilly's response and the teacher's fall from grace are shared with humor and insight. Of course, all's well that ends well. As in any Kevin Henkes illustrated endeavor, Lilly is a mouse and an exceptionally cute one at that!

Ketteman, Helen *Bubba the Cowboy Prince*

This Texas charmer is one of the best fractured versions of Cinderella around. Miss Lurleen throws a ball at her ranch in order to find the best cowpoke in Texas, someone to marry her and help her run the ranch. Bubba and his wicked stepbrothers, Duane and Milton, are up for the challenge except that Bubba gets a little extraordinary assistance from the local fairy godcow. Naturally, there's a happy ending. Reading this aloud is a romp, and the illustrations are as fun as Ketteman's text.

Lester, Helen *Hooway for Wodney Wat*

Rodney (or Wodney) is the underdog at school because he can't articulate his *r*'s. Things get even worse when a large rodent named Camilla Capybara joins the class. Camilla is an overbearing bully and makes life miserable for everyone. However, through an ingenious game of "Simon Says," Rodney sends Camilla off into the sunset forever and saves the school. "Hooway for Wodney Wat!" A must for children with speech delays, and just plain fun for the rest of us.

Lottridge, Celia Barker *The Name of the Tree* ❦

In this lyrical and beautiful retelling of a Bantu folktale, storyteller Celia Lottridge reveals that persistence and effort can save the day. When drought threatens to end their existence, the animals set out in search of something to eat. They discover a miraculous tree with strange and exotic fruit, but the tree will only lower its branches to those who know its name. The animals' quest is the story. Ian Wallace's stunning paintings are a magnificent backdrop to Lottridge's words, and his tree pulses with color and energy. The book has earned its place as a Canadian classic.

Meddaugh, Susan *Martha Speaks*

Martha the dog eats some alphabet soup, and the soup goes straight to her brain and gives her the ability to speak. Speak she does until her human family is fed up with all the talk and insults and lets her know that they would like her to return to being a "normal" dog. However, Martha's ability to speak ultimately saves the family from a late-night burglary, and Martha is welcomed back into the family fold, words and all. This is the first in the series of Martha books, which includes *Martha Blah Blah* and *Martha Walks the Dog*.

Morgan, Allen *Matthew and the Midnight Turkeys* ❦

Matthew and the Midnight Turkeys is the first and best of the Matthew series of Midnight Adventures. Matthew is a poor sleeper with a great imagination. When his mother gets up one morning to discover a major disaster in her kitchen, Matthew explains that the Midnight Turkeys caused the mess. He goes on to describe in detail the fabulous time he spent with the turkeys, including the singing of a sentimental song about underwear under a luminous streetlamp. His mother remains unconvinced. Michael Martchenko's comic nighttime paintings are at least half of the reason this book works so well and has endured so long.

Palatini, Margie *Piggie Pie*

Part fairy tale, part party, *Piggie Pie* is a rip-roaring read that takes flight along with Gritch the Witch and her search for pigs to put into her piggie pie. The book just gains speed, and the greedy but not overly bright witch and the wolf both get their just desserts in the end. Howard Fine's illustrations are bold, fast and expressive. Winner of many Children's Choice awards since it was published in 1995, this book is sure to be in demand to be read over and over again.

Stanley, Diane *Saving Sweetness*

A bone-rattling Western starring a hapless sheriff and the high-spirited and feisty orphan he rescues (along with the rest of the family!), *Saving Sweetness* is told in true western twang. It just aches to be read aloud and is sidesplittingly funny. Diane Stanley has certainly captured the spirit of the old West, and Brian Karas's dusty pictures are in perfect harmony with all the Texas talk. Don't forget to follow up on the sheriff's trials and tribulations in the sequel, *Raising Sweetness*.

Whybrow, Ian *Little Wolf's Book of Badness*

Little Wolf is just not very good at "big bad wolf behavior," and his parents pack him off to his uncle's school for rehabilitation and to earn his "badness" badge. His adventures on the way to and in school are relayed back to his parents in letter form and reveal that not all is what it seems! Little Wolf is an engaging character, and the finale of the book is hugely unanticipated and has great kid appeal (especially for boys of all ages). The design of the book complements the text very well, with attractive colors and sidebars containing additional humorous text.

Yolen, Jane *Sleeping Ugly*

Sleeping Ugly was initially conceived as a read-on-your-own vehicle for six- to eight-year-olds, but trust Jane Yolen to turn it into a mini-masterpiece of simple language. Loosely based on the tale of Sleeping Beauty, the story line employs many of the conventions of traditional fairy tales. It is a witty parody with great characters, including an utterly spoiled princess and an equally fed up fairy godmother with attitude. Pair this one with a traditional version of Sleeping Beauty. I usually use Trina Schart Hyman's.

> *Moral: Let sleeping princesses lie or lying*
> *princesses sleep, whichever seems wisest.*

Part III: *Sally Bender*

In choosing the books for this list, I went back to the experiences that I have daily with the children who come to the library for book shares. I am constantly on the lookout for books that will pique their interest, tickle their funny bone and show them what great teachers writers and illustrators can be. Writers and illustrators create characters whose actions inspire us to do better in our daily lives. They encourage our laughter and our love of language. They show us that we, too, can learn some of the lessons that they have learned as they strive to create new and breathtaking literature to be shared in our schools and homes. Their artistic talent is evident in their use of line, color and perspective, and in their ability to match their dazzling illustrations with fine text to ensure successful collaboration.

Aylesworth, Jim *Country Crossing*

Trains in the city seem more annoying than fascinating. They hold up traffic and cause minor delays whenever they run. In the country at night, however, they can provide a sensory experience second to none.

As the little old car putts toward the railroad crossing, the occupants hear all the night sounds that surround them. The crickets chirp, an owl hoots and the car's tires roll over the lonely country road. But when the car comes to a stop at the controlled crossing, the night sounds are obliterated by the clanging of the bell and the approach of a freight train. The train passes and peace is restored. The car moves across the tracks on its way home.

A trip for the senses and a journey back in time.

Bourgeois, Paulette *Franklin in the Dark* ✤

Paulette Bourgeois says she got the idea for this story while watching an episode of *M*A*S*H*. What a source of inspiration!

Franklin can do many things independently, but he is afraid of small, dark places. That fear is a real problem for a young turtle. His mother reassures him, but he cannot be dissuaded from his anxiety. So he seeks help. As he looks to overcome his fear, he finds that others are also afraid and they need help to face their own fears. When he finally meets up with his mother again, he sees that she has been afraid for him. Is everyone afraid of something? The final line is sheer delight and makes this my favorite Franklin story, hands down.

Ellis, Sarah *Big Ben* ❦

Being the youngest in the family can be a blessing, but it can also be a curse. Ben wants to be like his older siblings. He wants a report card. But they don't have subjects in preschool and they don't have report cards either. Furthermore, Ben can't swim, he can't read, he can't even see out the car windows. When his siblings notice Ben's misery, they make a decision. Taking him into their office, they fashion a report card that focuses on everything Ben does well. Straight A's for Ben and for Sarah Ellis. This is a terrific book.

Feiffer, Jules *I Lost My Bear*

The irreverent humor and cartoon characters have kids lapping up this wonderful story of a little girl who cannot find the bear that she needs before she settles down for the night. No one will help her. They offer suggestions, but they leave the detective work up to her. As she searches, her attention is drawn to all the other favorite toys that she does find. In the end, she forgets all about her bear . . . until BEDTIME! Now she is headed to bed without her favorite stuffed animal. What will she do?

Listeners love the dialogue and the angst that the child faces in her emotional search for her bear, and they delight in the embarrassment she feels when she discovers its hiding place.

Fitch, Sheree *Mabel Murple* ❦

Sheree Fitch calls it "lip-slippery" language and she is right! My kids love to watch my tongue get tangled as I read this poetic ode to the color purple. No matter how many times I read it, my tongue always betrays me.

The girl who loves purple does not even have a name when we first meet her. It seems only fitting that her name must rhyme with her favorite color. So we are introduced to Mabel Murple, who screams purple from every pore. Her house, her hair, her poodle are purple. She eats purple food and wears purple polka-dot pajamas. But what if her name were Gertrude Green?

Fitch, Sheree *No Two Snowflakes* ✤

Letters pass from one friend to another . . . one in Canada and one in Africa. How do you describe winter in Canada to someone who has never experienced it? Sheree Fitch uses her facility with language to do just that, and she does so in wonderful, descriptive text. We crunch through icy snow, breathe icicles in the cold Canadian air and make angels in the powdery snow. Can angels be made in sand? Can both friends be making their angels at the same time in different parts of the world? Beautiful language and matching beauty in the faces of the characters who play parts in this universal story of the children of the world.

Gay, Marie-Louise *Stella, Star of the Sea* ✤

You absolutely want to meet Stella and her little brother, Sam. Stella is the perfect "know-it-all" sister, and she is continually exasperated by Sam's questions. Sam is cautious and young, and he wants to be sure that Stella is not leading him astray.

In his first visit to the seashore, Sam is apprehensive. He wants to know all there is to know about his new surroundings. He has no intention of going into the water until his questions are answered and his anxiety eased. Stella is patient and persuasive. Finally, Sam launches himself into the water and floats like a noodle in a bowl of chicken soup. Now that he is in, will he ever come out?

Henkes, Kevin *Owen*

Owen is a young mouse who knows about love. He loves his blanket, Fuzzy. Fuzzy goes where Owen goes and likes what Owen likes. Everyone has an opinion to share about Owen's dependence on Fuzzy, especially his nosy neighbor.

Mrs. Tweezers mentions the Blanket Fairy, the vinegar trick and just saying "NO!" Nothing changes Owen's mind. With school starting soon, his parents become more concerned. But without Fuzzy, Owen is inconsolable. And then Mom has a splendid idea! Even Mrs. Tweezers can offer no argument.

Kevin Henkes knows young children . . . their fears, their joys and their foibles. If this is your first adventure with Kevin, please don't let it be your last.

Keefer, Janice Kulyk *Anna's Goat* ❦

Anna's Goat was inspired by a true story from World War II. Anna and her family are forced to leave their homeland and begin the hard life of the refugee. The parents must work, and the children are left with a nanny goat to keep them company. They must leave the goat behind when they return to their home, only to find it in ruins. As the children search the rubble for treasures that will remind them of better times, Anna chooses a scrap of cloth that had been nibbled by the nanny goat, and she finds comfort in her good memories. The realistic characters give life to this story and inspire admiration and concern for Anna and her family.

Koller, Jackie *No Such Thing*

A certain admonition is heard in many bedrooms at bedtime: There is nothing to fear in the darkness! There are no such things as monsters! Imagine Monster's surprise when his mother tells him that there are no such things as boys after he expresses his own bedtime fears.

Get ready for hilarity as each discovers the other and comes to know the truth of the matter. They laugh together and cry. They worry and fret. Finally, they decide that they have a lesson to teach their respective mothers. I guarantee the reading will be followed with a resounding "Read it again!"

Lee, Dennis *Bubblegum Delicious* ❦

From the first poem in this collection, I am taken back to the joy of sharing Dennis Lee's *Alligator Pie* with our kids when they were young. They loved the lilting rhymes and the hilarious situations that the poet created with his words. In this more recent book, Lee returns to the rhythmic fun of an earlier time.

Two intrepid adventurers stalk the neighborhood in search of shared experiences. They meet a worthy cast of characters and feast their eyes upon many of nature's wonders. Their engaging and tender verses are countered by the feisty and irreverent interjections of a bevy of boisterous bugs.

Lunn, Janet *The Umbrella Party* ❈

Christie loves umbrellas more than anything else in the world. When it is time for her birthday, she tells her friends that the only thing she wants is an umbrella. Her friends are appalled and decide to teach her a lesson. They each buy an umbrella. Christie is thrilled!

Her greatest joy is her grandfather's gift, a brilliant, gargantuan beach umbrella, the perfect excuse to move the party to the beach. There the partygoers learn the value of the umbrella, and Christie is triumphant.

Kady MacDonald Denton's expressive characters and colorful array of umbrellas add the perfect touch to this gently humorous story of one young girl's obsession. Proof positive that umbrellas play an important role in the grand scheme of things.

Morgan, Allen *Sadie and the Snowman* ❈

Sadie is determined to build a snowman. She uses all her skill to roll the three snowballs and to decorate her creation with appropriate accoutrements. Her work is detailed and the snowman lasts a long time. Eventually, however, warm sunshine and hungry animals bring him to an end. Undeterred, Sadie tries again. And again. Each time, her snowman succumbs to the brilliance of the sunshine and the hunger of the neighborhood critters.

When the weather warms, Sadie knows just what to do to ensure that her friend will return with the cold of the next winter sky. Young listeners enjoy the determination with which Sadie faces the task of snowman building. The repetitive events help them predict the outcome, and they are intrigued by Sadie's persistence.

Munsch, Robert *The Paper Bag Princess* ❈

Elizabeth is a young woman to be admired. She is not deterred when a loathsome dragon burns her castle and carries off her beloved. She is resolute in her quest to find the dragon and her betrothed. When she comes to his castle, the dragon is unwilling to hear her request. He has been busy eating and his stomach is full. Elizabeth will not be put off. She demands an audience.

With false praise and an appeal to the dragon's power, Elizabeth is able to trick him into submission. She rescues Ronald, who proves to be unworthy of such a splendid woman. And she unceremoniously dumps him . . . a perfect ending to a modern fairy tale.

Rankin, Joan *Wow! It's Great Being a Duck*

Lillie is the last born and the smallest. Her mother loves her to distraction. But Lillie is not like her brothers and sisters. She does not want to take her feet from the ground, an improbable characteristic in a small white duck. Her mother tries to warn her about the fox, but Lillie will not be convinced of the danger.

She ventures out into the forest, still encumbered by a piece of shell that blocks her sight. When she meets the fox, she is oblivious to his wily ways. Only when she is faced with the real danger of being eaten do Lillie's basic instincts take over and bring her to safety. Wow, it's great being a duck!

This is a perfect book to help young readers understand many of the strategies that authors and illustrators use as they develop a story and produce a worthy book. In this story, children can be introduced to sound effects, changing fonts, use of italics, description, humor, foreshadowing and great excitement. They also observe use of white space, changing perspectives, speech bubbles and movement in the art that has been created to enhance the text. Add to that it is a book worthy of repeated readings, and you have a winner from start to finish.

Steig, William *Sylvester and the Magic Pebble*

Steig's books are among my favorite read alouds for all ages, adults included. He writes for children with an unwavering belief in their ability to comprehend sophisticated language and story lines. In this book, we meet a loving family of donkeys whose son disappears when he finds a magic red pebble, the perfect addition to his ever-growing collection of remarkable specimens.

Sylvester recognizes the power of the pebble, but unwittingly becomes the victim of its magic when he is frightened by the approach of a mean and hungry lion. The remainder of the story tells of the distraught parents as they search high and low for their beloved son. A fortunate turn of events at a spring picnic releases Sylvester from his magical prison and all is well.

Tregebov, Rhea *The Big Storm* ✤

No Manitoban worth her salt could fail to include this fine book in a list of favorites. Set in a Jewish delicatessen on Winnipeg's Selkirk Avenue, it introduces us to Jeanette and her family. Everyone has a job at the deli, including Jeanette's cat, Kitty Doyle. She is a talented mouser. Her other job is to walk Jeanette to and from school each day. After spirited play in new-fallen snow at the end of a school day, Jeanette is enticed to visit Polly's house with a promise of warm latkes. All the while, Kitty Doyle waits patiently in the cold.

Jeanette is distraught when she remembers her loyal friend, and warm milk and unwavering love together ensure Kitty Doyle's survival. The warmth of the deli and the bracing cold of a Winnipeg storm are evident in Maryann Kovalski's spirited and detailed watercolors. Bravo!

Turney-Zagwÿn, Deborah *Hound Without Howl*

The wordplay adds just the right touch of humor to this book about a man and his hound. Howard is a bachelor who loves the opera, and he is looking for a companion who loves music. When he finds Clayton, a bassett hound, he is sure that he has found the perfect dog—but Clayton only wags his tail. There is no baying, even for his good friend. Will the friendship last?

Turney-Zagwÿn, Deborah *Long Nellie* ✤

What a character study this book proves to be! We first meet Long Nellie, a lonely outcast, as she collects wood for her stove. Jeremy's mother tells him that Nellie is a scavenger. She takes what others throw away. She seems the perfect person, then, to take care of a squirming, scruffy cat that Jeremy finds hidden in a garbage can in his garage. Now he must find a way to introduce the two. In so doing, Jeremy inadvertently becomes acquainted with the cheerful and caring Nellie, and a friendship blossoms. The cat is in good hands and Jeremy has learned a valuable lesson in tolerance for those who do not always fit the mold.

Long Nellie was as thin as a curved
rake and as tall as a bent stepladder.

Viorst, Judith *Alexander, Who Used to Be Rich Last Sunday*

Alexander, Nicholas and Anthony, those beloved brothers, are the recipients of cash from their grandparents during a weekend visit. Each receives a dollar. One week later, Alexander is lamenting the fact that his brothers have cash left, and all he has are . . . bus tokens. We are taken on a whirlwind trip as Alexander parts with the cash that last Sunday was his. Bubblegum, bets, a snake rental and bad language aimed at his brothers make quick work of more than half of it. You get the picture!

Now Alexander is left to discover a way to make some money so that he has something left to save. What fun and what a lesson to learn!

What fun to use great literature to help young learners find out about math concepts! I use this book in teachers' workshops and in math classes. Be sure that you have the coins that they will need to help them discover how much money Nicholas and Anthony have left, and also the coins that Alexander will need as he goes on his spending spree. Many young children have no concept of money; this story can help them develop an interest and understand how money disappears. Using real money adds authenticity. Children will read the story again and again as they make real-life connections.

Part iv: *Lucie Poulin-Mackey*

Picture books and easy-reading novels abound in this list. Books that can move with words and pictures are essential at this age level. Children will often use picture clues to understand what they are reading. They start using this strategy with picture books and carry on with heavily illustrated to easy-reading novels. Picture books are essential in a child's collection and a must in the classroom. The books that I've chosen for this list are great read alouds. As educators we sometimes forget the joy of being read to. By reading aloud to our students or children on a daily basis, we not only give them the example of a good reader; also we provide them with rich and worthwhile literature.

Base, Graeme *Le point d'eau*

This ecological tale set in a magical marshland deep in a secret forest will captivate all that read it. Each page includes a species of animal from around the world that comes to drink from the magical source. With comical frogs as guides, the reader explores the range of ecosystems found on our precious earth. The book is masterfully illustrated with Graeme Base's spectacular watercolors. As the story progresses, the waterhole becomes smaller and smaller till it is gone. But hope is on the horizon. A beautiful read-aloud book.

Dix kangourous regardaient la mare. Il n'y avait rien à dire. L'eau avait disparu.

Davidts, Jean-Pierre *L'ABC du roi Léon* ❦

King Léon has lost his secretary when he needs her most. He needs to issue a decree and has no choice but to write it himself. He asks the royal teacher to review his message before he sends it throughout his kingdom, only to be told, "Your royal majesty, you must go back to school. Your need to review your ABC's." Will the king return to school? And will he ever write his message? It is very important!

This story is a wonderful read to help students understand the importance of learning the alphabet.

Demers, Dominique *Vieux Thomas et la petite fée* ❦

This modern twist to Beauty and the Beast is a beautiful story of selflessness. Old Thomas finds a tiny lifeless girl lying on the beach. She is no bigger than a match. For several days and several nights he keeps her warm and tries to feed her. When he thinks that all hope is gone, a miracle happens. Together they find new life.

All is well until the fateful day when Thomas goes fishing as he does every day, only to feel that something isn't right. He rushes home to find a wolf in the house. Battle ensues and the strongest one wins. Thomas has expired. What will happen to the little fairy?

> *À la tombée du jour, il se leva péniblement et marcha lentement vers la mer. C'est là qu'il souhaitait disparaître, parmi les poissons aux écailles lumineuses et les coquillages enfouis.*

Ferraris, Nathalie *La picotte du vendredi soir* ❧

Could a person get chicken pox from watching television? Nathalie thinks so. And through her unusual imagination, the reader begins to wonder. In Nathalie's favorite television show, the twins have chicken pox. Soon Nathalie has symptoms just like theirs. Only the doctor can tell what is wrong with Nathalie.

This is a hilarious tale that will have everyone in stitches.

Graham, Georgia *Le jour de la tornade*
French text by Pierre Bertrand ❧

This story was inspired by the true story of the Reid family in Cremona, Alberta, whose farm was devastated by a tornado in 1965. The reader is immersed in the tension that builds in the story and through the pictures. The clouds build; the wind picks up speed. Then the tornado hits and each family member must find shelter. What noise! What debris! Luckily they find each other after the storm. Now they must begin the task of cleaning up and beginning a new life. An important Canadian story. A must for all personal libraries.

> *Durant ce qui leur paraît un siècle, le père et le fils voient défiler à toute vitesse, devant leur ouverture, de la poussière, du foin et des branches.*

Greenburg, Dan *Zack voit double*
French text by Olivier de Broca

Zack is a normal boy who lives in New York City, but he has unusual adventures. This is just one of them. While trying to take his retainer out of the bathroom cabinet one night, Zack meets his reflection. It is alive and well and in his bathroom. Adventures follow. After reading this story, the reader is invited to play games in a supplement provided in the back. A story that all will enjoy, boys and girls.

Harrison, Troon *Le chasseur de rêves*
French text by Christiane Duchesne ✾

I first bought this book to help my oldest son, Sébastien, with his bad-dream phase. After reading this book, his dreams grew less frequent and less scary.

In the story, Zacharie wakes up knowing that this will be a special day. For weeks now a big dog and two zebras have been drinking from the birdbath in the backyard. An old man is in the neighborhood with his truck, which bears the words "The Dream Collector." That's odd, thinks Zacharie. Apparently, a municipal bylaw forbids dreams from being abroad during the day. But the truck is breaking down, and dreams are running amok. Zacharie's ready to help, but time is running out. A feel-good book for all.

Levert, Mireille *Une île dans la soupe* ✾

This story takes place at mealtime and evokes strong memories of childhood play. Victor's wild imagination is awakened by the wonderful smell of Mom's soup. The brave knight has a dangerous task to perform, eating Mom's fish soup. "Look, there's an island in my soup!" he cries and the adventure begins. Witches, dragons and carrot-rain abound. Mireille Levert won the Governor General's Literary Award for Illustrations for this book.

For the knight in your life.

Lewis, Rose *Mon bébé du bout du monde*
French text by Françoise Mateu

An excellent read for adopted children, especially from overseas. The anticipation and the wait are clearly stated by the mother-to-be. This story is told by her to her daughter. The mother tells her daughter just how much she wanted her and that she had to promise to care for her.

The first moments of the little girl's arrival are simply but beautifully described. Love emanates from every page.

Pef *La belle lisse poire du prince de Motordu*

This is a French classic. The Prince of Motordu (twisted words) leads a comfortable life in his castle with all that goes along with a royal life. One small problem threatens to ruin it all: he has a speech impediment that causes him to mix his letters. A *mouton* (sheep) becomes a *bouton* (button). His parents despair that he will ever marry, but as luck would have it he does meet a fair maiden (who happens to be a teacher). A story of love, wordplay and all-round fun. You will find the prince in all sorts of other adventures as well.

> *Il habitait un chapeau magnifique au-dessus*
> *duquel, le dimanche, flottaient des crapauds*
> *bleu blanc rouge, qu'on pouvait voir de loin.*

I love to laugh and play with words and to share that joy with my children and my students in order to demystify our beautiful language, its complexities and its glories. *La belle lisse poire du prince de Motordu* plays with words in ways that help our children appreciate the beauty and magic of our language. I hope you have as much fun with it as I had.

Piquemal, Michel *La poule qui pond des patates*

What good is a chicken if she can't lay eggs? The chicken is given an ultimatum. If she doesn't start to lay, into the casserole she will go. In an effort to stay alive, she finds all sorts of things to replace the eggs she doesn't produce. The perfect story to tickle your funny bone.

Pow, Tom *Regarde autour de toi*
French text by Hélène Souchon

Here I go again. Another family relationship book, masterfully illustrated. This one creates parallels between the animal world and the people world in an exploration of father/son relationships. I haven't been able to read it aloud yet because I know I'll cry.

From the forest to the jungle to the depths of the ocean, sons ask, "Who does this belong to?" And for every beautiful description of land and sea and skies comes the same reply, "Look around. This is all for you." Keep the tissues handy. To call this book a tearjerker is an understatement.

Pour qui est la terre? demande un petit garçon à son père alors qu'ils sont tous deux enroulés dans une chaude couverture.

Rémillard-Bélanger, Julie *Alasi, Jimmy et la mer*
Inuktitut by Sarah Beaulne ❋

What an homage to one of this nation's founding people, the Inuit! The story is written in French on one page and in Inuktitut on the opposite page. A great way for our children to learn of this culture.

Alasi, Jimmy's father, is a fisherman. Every night he tells his family of his adventures, introducing them to the animals of the sea, from the whales to the seals, from the bears to the birds. Come and learn of these people, their language, their way of life, their heritage and their way of preserving it.

Simard, Danielle *L'animal secret* ❋

Louis's mom is a biologist. One night, while he's in bed, he overhears a conversation she has on the telephone. He discovers that Mom must deal with a monster. What kind of monster could it be? And what does Mom have to do with it? Must she destroy it? Questions, questions and more questions he asks himself while trying to sleep. A good book about a wild imagination. Also a good book about a mother and son relationship.

Tibo, Gilles *Le camping du petit géant* ❋

Sylvain is a little boy with a big imagination. Every book is a big adventure that ends in Sylvain's parents' bed. In this book, Sylvain goes camping for the first time, and the adventure moves to the great outdoors. At first all is well, but soon raccoons become ferocious beasts and mosquitoes become terrifying. An easy read for beginning readers. You will find plenty of other adventures in the series.

CHAPTER FOUR

Nine- to Eleven-Year-Olds

Part 1: *David Bouchard*

Our Canadian and American schools expect children in this age group to be reading. Actually, expect is too mild; demand is more accurate. Once they reach the age of nine, or sooner, children are no longer allowed to read at their own pace for pleasure. I've seen a child in grade three break into tears after learning that she had been classified as a level three reader. She had expected to be recognized as a level one reader.

Adults — what are we doing to our children? Why are we robbing them of these early years of reading pleasure? They will not get another chance! Allow your children to continue to love books and reading. Do not buy into the notion that we must use whatever methods are available to get children reading earlier and earlier, all for one purpose, to achieve.

There is no end to the number of books that can captivate your children. Let them fall in love. They deserve to want to read . . . they deserve to love reading. And frankly, you deserve to be right there next to them, part of what can be a life-altering experience.

It is in the spirit of allowing children to read in their own good time that you'll find a selection of picture books and books that are easy to read in the following lists. At this stage, strong readers will move up into the next list, and that is wonderful. Allow your children to set the pace, fast or slow. Do not push your children.

Avi *The True Confessions of Charlotte Doyle*

I have too many of Avi's books on my lists — I know that. But this is one of Avi's books that children love, even hard-to-please boys like me. This story of a young girl's adventures on the high seas has something that appeals to us non-fiction types who always relish history and adventure that lets us travel the world.

Babbitt, Natalie *Tuck Everlasting*

The Tuck family has discovered the source of eternal life. When one of the Tuck boys falls in love, he offers his beloved the choice between a normal life ending in death and the chance to be with him forever. The movie is amazing and yet, as it is so often said, it's not as good as the book. Those of us who read the book prior to seeing the movie will tell you that we loved it then and that we love it now. Children's books can allow readers into unknown worlds: the future, the past, magic and in this case, a world of life everlasting, inhabited by the lucky (or not so lucky) Tucks.

Boston, Lucy *The Children of Green Knowe*

Green Knowe is a house, a garden and a lifestyle in the most spectacular setting Britain has to offer. Lucy Boston, who started writing at the age of sixty-three, bought Green Knowe, one of the oldest lived-in homes in Britain, and began writing this amazing series, focusing on the history of the property as seen through the eyes of children who have lived in the house over the centuries. Most children who grew up in Britain during the 1960s have read Lucy Boston's books. Her characters, her stories and her success all begin with this amazing house. This series is what a series can and should be: more, please.

> I've been to Green Knowe. The house is exactly as Lucy Boston describes it. The garden is everything she describes it to be and more. My girls and I were blessed to discover it during a home exchange in Britain. To say that the characters and indeed the entire series came more fully alive for us on our visit to Green Knowe is an understatement. We fell in love with the countryside, the house and everything that relates to this delightful series.

Dahl, Roald *Revolting Rhymes*

This collection of rhymes written in the most clever and disgusting of ways is every young boy's favorite. I've known girls to like it as well.

During his lifetime, Dahl was accused of many things, including ageism, but he was never accused of failing to captivate his young audiences. *Revolting Rhymes* has always been my favorite. This book is a must, particularly for boys.

Dahl, Roald *The Twits*

Mr. and Mrs. Twit are the most revolting couple in the world. Their lives, relationship and adventure are enough to make most adults sick. Kids love it. Here I go again . . . a repeat author. But how not? Dahl's crude language need not be restricted to poetry; it works equally well in prose. My favorite of Dahl's novels is *The Twits*. It is a guaranteed winner when read aloud, at least with ten-year-old boys.

Gardiner, John Reynolds *Stone Fox*

Can there be a gentler theme than "a boy and his dog"? Add to that an orphan boy with a sick grandfather for whom he must win a crucial dogsled race, and look out—get out the tissues. This book is not a masterpiece. It is merely a touching read that is sure to draw a tear from most of us—even on third and fourth readings.

Harrison, Michael and Christopher Stuart-Clark (Compilers) *The Oxford Treasury of Classic Poems*

Poetry needs to be a big part of your collection. It is too easy to neglect poetry in favor of the more straightforward world of prose. However, you must work to include poetry consistently. Anthologies are a good way of accomplishing this goal. This collection is one of many that are available. The poems are well selected and appeal to many age groups.

Herriot, James *James Herriot's Animal Stories*

How can I go from the harsh imagery and crude language of Roald Dahl to the work of James Herriot? Herriot is to children's books what Martha Stewart is to North American homes. He is simply good! James Herriot's charming stories of a vet's experiences in the English countryside are gentle and wholesome. And this series is beautifully illustrated. Animal stories work equally well with girls as with boys.

Little, Jean *From Anna* ❋

Jean Little is one of Canada's foremost children's writers. I could have selected any one of a number of her books, but chose this one because of its message. Parents and children need to be reminded of the many disabilities that can affect a child's ability to read and write. Anna's disability is poor eyesight. Once her poor vision is diagnosed and dealt with, all is well. But before that, Anna, who immigrates to Canada from Germany in the 1930s, is confronted with the frustrations that so many of our children live with from day to day.

Lurie, Alison (Editor) *The Oxford Book of Modern Fairy Tales*

Another anthology filled with little treasures. This collection is a perfect grouping of short stories that focus on the role of women in folklore, fantasy and fairy tales. My favorite is "The Princess Who Stood on Her Own Two Feet." Many of these fairy tales have strong messages that all girls should hear again and again, preferably while they are young and impressionable.

Montgomery, Lucy Maud *Anne of Green Gables* ❋

Is there anyone in Canada who has not followed the touching adventures of the little red-haired orphan girl, Anne Shirley, and her older adopted parents from P.E.I.? You know why your children should meet her. Anne tends to appeal to girls more than to boys, but if she is presented in the right way at the right time, boys can grow to love her too. This is as good a time as any to include television or movies in your reading program. Watching Anne on the big screen made me want to read the books.

Nixon, Joan Lowery *The Orphan Train Adventures* series

Joan Lowery Nixon has won many prestigious awards for her writing for children. I particularly like this series that touches on the life of a family of orphan children in times that were less than easy. Nixon moves us nicely from passage to passage within the series, holding our interest and driving us to want more. This is what series writing should be, and this is the age when our children are most eager to seek out books in series.

Park, Barbara *Mick Harte Was Here*

Authors who can make us laugh the way that Park does in her Junie B. Jones books are usually also blessed with the ability to make us cry. Nothing could be better proof of this than Barbara's touching look at a teenage girl trying to cope with the death of her little brother. All children's collections should include books that comfort and give children a place to go when life deals hard blows, such as the death of a pet, friend or family member. *Mick Harte Was Here* is one of those comfort zones, if and when needed. It sure feels good to us adults as well.

> *I stood up and looked at it. I smiled. Mick Harte was here. And now he's gone. But for twelve years and five months, my brother was one of the neatest kids you'd ever want to meet. And I just wanted to tell you about him, that's all. I just thought you ought to know.*

Park, Barbara *Skinnybones*

There is no better read aloud for ten-year-olds than *Skinnybones*. In the story, a young boy discovers himself through a series of life experiences, mostly in the classroom and on the baseball field. If you have any ten-year-olds in your life, this is likely to be the single best gift I'm able to offer you. Read it. And once you're done, seek out *Almost Starring Skinnybones*, the sequel. It is not quite as good, but almost!

It was not all that many years ago that, as the newest member of an administrative team in a British Columbia senior secondary school, I was made responsible for a goodly number of students who, for various reasons, were unable to cope in the regular school system. After sharing with them the fact that, because of my relatively sheltered upbringing, we had little in common, I told them that I had recently discovered the world of children's books. I then informed them that I'd be reading to them for 45 minutes per week. After a few rude comments on their part, I began reading *Skinnybones*. I was reading this grade three/four book to students in their late teens. Though they didn't say they liked it, they did call to ask me why I wasn't coming in to read to them when I was at home sick with the stomach flu. It is that good a read! Do not miss reading it aloud. You owe it to yourself and to your children. (Girls are apt to enjoy *Beanpole* in much the same way.)

Paulsen, Gary *Dunc Culpepper* series

You'd think that I would be growing tired of categorizing books based on the interest of boys and girls, but it is hard for me not to. Grade four boys love the adventures of young Dunc Culpepper. The series covers holidays, vacations and everyday events. I have read this series time and time again to children in grades two to five and it is always a hit! Gary Paulsen has always been one of my favorite writers. He gave me a great thrill when he came to speak to my students in West Vancouver, B.C.

Part II: *Anne Letain*

This has to be the coming-of-age list. Almost without exception, the protagonists in this group of titles are dealing with the issues of growing up and becoming independent, actualized young people. Whether through adventure (*The Ear, the Eye and the Arm, Kensuke's Kingdom*), personal tribulation (*Dust, Walk Two Moons, Awake and Dreaming*) or humor (*The Nose from Jupiter, Harris and Me, A Long Way from Chicago*), each character, male and female alike, gains insight into what it means to become more grown up.

These books explore that special time between childhood and adulthood when young people encounter some of the graver realities of life and often have to dig deep into their psyches to find solutions and responses. With their rich renderings of early adolescence, these authors have never lost the feeling of what it like to be eleven or twelve years old. There is a feast of good reading to be found here and an opportunity to explore the essential innocence of this age group.

Almond, David *Skellig*

Skellig is an unforgettable and remarkable read. Original and haunting, it is Michael's story of the discovery of a mysterious stranger in his family's garage. While the rest of the family is concerned with his baby sister's

illness, Michael is obsessed with and consumed by the strange creature —
part bird, part angel, perhaps. In considered and tender language, Almond
has created a universal tale about the fragility of life.

Butcher, Kristin *The Gramma War* 🍁

An elderly, cranky, unrepentant smoker of a grandmother comes to live
with Annie and her family. Annie's family is the archetypal Canadian
four-member family, but how Kristin Butcher handles the situation is
not typical. There are no easy fixes or solutions or even happy endings
to the problems Annie and her family face. This is a realistic novel for
kids that really works because it is readily identifiable and close to home
for many children. Without diminishing the magnitude of the dilemma,
Butcher applies gentle humor and keen observation and delivers the
goods. *The Gramma War* teaches but doesn't preach.

Creech, Sharon *Walk Two Moons*

Salamanca Hiddle's mother has disappeared without explanation, and
this mystery is the huge central hole in Sal's life. Her grandparents decide
to take Sal on an extended road trip to help her cope. Eventually the
past and the present come together in a revelation of the truth. Engross-
ing and richly emotional, the story keeps the reader hanging in, guessing until the end. A deserving winner of the Newbery Medal and many
other international awards, Sharon Creech is an author to be turned to
again and again.

Curtis, Christopher Paul
The Watsons Go to Birmingham — 1963

Meet the weird Watsons of Flint, Michigan — Momma, Dad, Byron
(official juvenile delinquent), Kenny and little sister, Joetta. Because of
Byron's proclivities, Momma and Dad decide that it's time for a little
butt kicking with Grandma in Birmingham, Alabama. Their car trip
collides with one of the bleakest moments of American history. At once
warm, comic and moving, this is an inviting and evocative story of a
truly memorable family. The book has won numerous Kids' Choice
awards around the continent.

Farmer, Nancy *The Ear, the Eye and the Arm*

Zimbabwe, 2194. General Matsika's three children steal out of the family compound on a forbidden adventure and vanish. Their frantic parents hire the most unlikely of detectives: the Ear, the Eye and the Arm. Each of the detectives has special mutated powers to assist them in their quest to find the children. This high and quirky adventure features adept characterization and witty dialogue. The book just zips along to its very satisfying conclusion.

Gantos, Jack *Jack's Black Book*

Jack Gantos's remembrances of a misspent childhood in Florida are immortalized in *Jack's Black Book*. Comprising three novellas, each of which stands alone, the book as a whole constitutes a hilarious re-creation of Jack's life in seventh grade. Jack's wish to be a writer provides the impetus for his recording the consequences of flunking an IQ test and explaining how, among other things, he got his toe tattooed. Some adults may find Jack's antics hard to take, but *Jack's Black Book* is a great giggle for most middle schoolers. If you need more Jack, there's *Jack on the Tracks*, *Heads or Tails* and *Jack's New Power*.

> Fifteen nine-year-old boys and I got together to discuss *Jack's Black Book*. More than a few adults are not as enamored of Jack and his adventures as I am. I started the discussion with a quote from a reviewer who was not impressed. My boys took the review almost personally. Didn't the reviewer know that boys really like gross? One particularly precocious lad even coined a new word to describe the book — "vomitrocious." Worthy of consideration for the *Oxford Canadian Dictionary*, I'd say! I've replaced the "Jack" books at least once, and they all seem to have a habit of going missing forever!

Hesse, Karen *The Music of Dolphins*

Deceptively simply written, *The Music of Dolphins* tells the story of Mila, a feral child who has been raised by dolphins since the age of four. She is returned to the human fold where zealous researchers teach her language and music and other human activities that are not quite so high-minded. This is a book that lingers for a long time as the reader reflects on and re-examines what it means to be human. Unforgettable in its simplicity, this is a book that can be equally meaningful to a nine-year-old or an adult.

Ibbotson, Eva *Journey to the River Sea*

The story of the orphaned Maia's adventure to Manaus, a fabled Brazilian city a thousand miles from the mouth of the Amazon river, is an amazing yarn. Peopled with eccentric characters and traditional orphan problems, *Journey to the River Sea* is almost farcical, with a high quotient of tragedy thrown in for good measure. It is a rollicking read enhanced by Ibbotson's natural wittiness and warmth.

Jennings, Paul *Unreal!*

Welcome to the wild and wacky world of Paul Jennings and the first of his "UN" series of books. *Unreal!* is a compilation of eight stories that only Paul Jennings could dream up. Explore a haunted toilet in "The Ghost on the Dunny," find out why all the girls would want to kiss you in "Lucky Lips" and discover what it's like to run home in the nude in "Wunderpants." Paul Jennings is considered a national treasure among young readers in Australia. If you want more fearless stories check into *Unbelievable*, *Uncanny*, *Unbearable* and more.

Levine, Karen *Hana's Suitcase* ❦

Hana's Suitcase is a true story of the Holocaust spanning six decades and three continents, with a unique Canadian connection. It is the story of Hana Brady, a young Czech Jew who was first transported to the Terezin holding camp and ultimately to the death showers of Auschwitz. Levine's sensitive retelling of Hana's story never dwells on the atrocities, but young readers will gain an appreciation for and an understanding of a period in our history that we cannot afford to forget. The story is rendered even more memorable by the inclusion of original photographs that remarkably survived the war.

Morpurgo, Michael *Kensuke's Kingdom*

Fascinated by *Treasure Island* and *Robinson Crusoe* as a child, Michael Morpurgo had always wished to write a survival story. *Kensuke's Kingdom* is that book. Protagonist Michael's parents decide that the three of them will sail around the world after Michael's father's job is declared redundant. Somewhere in the South Seas, Michael and his dog, Stella Artois, are washed overboard. Washed ashore, they find themselves sharing an island with Kensuke, a Japanese soldier who never returned home after World War II. Kensuke becomes Michael's mentor to young manhood. Morpurgo shines with this sensitive and optimistic novel.

Paulsen, Gary *Harris and Me: A Summer Remembered*

During a postwar summer long ago, an eleven-year-old city boy is dumped with some farm relatives because of his parents' drinking problems. His nine-year-old cousin, Harris, is rude, crude and already an expert at finding trouble. Soon Harris leads his unsuspecting cousin into what can only be described as serious mischief. In *Harris and Me*, the prolific Gary Paulsen proves himself a top-notch humorist, but at the same time he never loses contact with the bittersweet circumstances of his narrator as he remembers his life that particular summer.

Pearson, Kit *Awake and Dreaming* ❧

Acclaimed Canadian children's writer Kit Pearson strikes gold once again with this compelling and dramatic page-turner. Theo, trapped in poverty with her young irresponsible mother, dreams of belonging to a real family with all the trappings. Her fantasy seems to come true when she is adopted by the Kaldors. Or did it really happen? This is a spellbinding ghost story; girls in particular will be attracted to it. It will wreak emotional havoc with the most hardened of readers.

Peck, Richard *A Long Way from Chicago*

Joey (the narrator) and his younger sister, Mary Alice, live in Chicago during the Depression. Every summer they go downstate to visit Grandma Dowdel. Grandma is way bigger than life, and she continually astounds her citified grandchildren with her incredible schemes to even the score with various members of the community. Consisting of eight hilarious but interrelated short stories, *A Long Way from Chicago* is storytelling at its finest.

Scrimger, Richard *The Nose from Jupiter* 🍁

Allan Dingwall is your very average thirteen-year-old. He is coping with his parents' divorce, his fascination with a particular girl in class and also with the fact that he's not too spectacular at much of anything. His worldview changes when an alien named Norbert takes up residence in his nose. Allan develops a whole new way of dealing with his life — with hilarious and often unbelievable consequences. Richard Scrimger is a relatively new voice in children's literature and is not to be missed. Don't overlook the sequels: *Nose for Adventure* and *Noses Are Red*.

> *Don't you hate it when everyone in the room is wearing clothes and you're not?*

Slade, Arthur *Dust* 🍁

When seven-year-old Matthew disappears on his first walk alone into the town near his home, it is up to Robert, his eleven-year-old brother, to solve the mystery of his disappearance. The story is set in the uncompromising dirty thirties of the Canadian prairies, and the first suspect is an uncanny stranger with shaman-like abilities. In *Dust*, Art Slade exquisitely explores the cusp between fantasy and reality and leaves the reader gasping. The language is reflective, emotional and brims with lovely imagery.

> *Dust* is most often used with the junior high crowd, but I liked it so much that I wanted to expose it to our nine- and ten-year-olds in my school. The kids absolutely loved it too. So when I had a chance to have Art Slade visit the school and our students, I was thrilled. Art began by reading from the first chapter of *Dust*. All of a sudden a quiet rumble began in the crowd. Art didn't know that there were thirty or more copies of the book in the students' hands, and they were following along closely with him. After other school visits, Art had taken the liberty of "editing" his own work so that it was less lengthy and would fit shorter attention spans. He was surprised when my students caught him out in his ruse and pleased when they objected to him leaving out words!

Part III: *Sally Bender*

It is uniquely challenging to find picture books that evoke spontaneous discussion with this age group. The text needs to be sophisticated enough to hold their interest, with a touch of humor, if possible. The humor often begins the talk, but children can be drawn toward larger issues if given the time and opportunity to voice their ideas, opinions and concerns.

Baylor, Byrd *I'm in Charge of Celebrations*

This book introduced me to the beautiful lyric prose of Byrd Baylor. Although no part of me wants to live in the desert with her, I admire her love of the world that surrounds her and her ability to describe it with such passion and clarity. In this book, she chooses not to commemorate the traditional days celebrated worldwide. Rather, she gives herself 108 celebrations.

In her notebook, she tracks each one, and she only places there those days that she will remember for the rest of her life: Dust Devil Day or Rainbow Celebration Day or Green Cloud Day, among others. She tells us that we will know those days that are to be celebrated by the pounding in our hearts and the luck we have in noticing them. For each of us, these celebrations will be different. What a way to look at the world!

Birdseye, Tom *Airmail to the Moon*

I keep one of my son's wisdom teeth in my pocket when I tell this story. Ora Mae Cotton is fixin' to cause a heap of trouble for anyone, and everyone, who might have stolen her tooth. It was a long time comin' out, that first tooth, and now it's missing. She embarks on a search, checking with every family member to be sure that they don't have it. No luck! Her ire is spent and the crying all done when Ora Mae discovers that her tooth is exactly where she left it!

Great colloquial speech makes this a perfect book for storytelling. Kids love Ora Mae's tenacity as she sets out to find the culprit who took the tooth, and her embarrassment when she discovers that all her caterwaulin' has been for nought.

Bouchard, David *Voices from the Wild* 🍁

No book of David's has more impact on the kids at my school than this one. I love to read it and they love to guess the animal that I am describing. The fact that David has shared parts of it while visiting with us has had a huge impact as well. Children listen attentively to the plea of each animal as it tries to convince the artist to paint its portrait. And each has good reason to be the one chosen.

The lyric voice of the poet shines through in every poem. He has much to share with his readers, and he shares it in a sensually stimulating way, inviting us to know more than we have ever known about the animals chosen for their remarkable abilities. At the end, he provides thumbnail reports on each animal, adding to our store of information. To hear him "rap" each piece is the icing on the cake. I will continue to look forward to a taped rendition of the "voices" that only David can provide.

Brisson, Pat *The Summer My Father Was Ten*

I use this story every year with our older kids to give them experience with memoir writing, taking an event in their life that has been life-changing and giving it voice.

When the author's father was ten, he and his friends were playing ball when their ball went into a neighbor's garden. In the excitement of the moment, the boys did something that they had not set out to do. When confronted by the gardener, most of the boys are embarrassed but not apologetic. Only the father is contrite. His feelings of remorse plague him until he finally does something about it.

This book is a wonderful vehicle for discussion and will lead listeners to consider a time in their lives that might be remembered always.

Browne, Anthony *Voices in the Park*

I hope this is not your first Anthony Browne book, but if it is, I know it will not be your last. He is a brilliant writer and illustrator.

This story is told in four voices, from differing perspectives. An uppity mother and her s'mother'ed son enter the park at the same time as a gruff father and his very friendly young daughter. Both families have dogs. The dogs get along famously, and the children learn to like each other, but the parents have no interest in altering their own perceptions. Changing fonts match the shifting seasons as each narrator tells his/her own version of the events that they share. There is so much to see on each illustrated page. You will pore over it again and again.

Edwards, Pamela Duncan
Barefoot: Escape on the Underground Railroad

As we watch Barefoot travel the path that is part of the Underground Railroad, we note that the animals have a part to play in his bid for freedom. The heron announces his approach, the frog helps him find water to quench his thirst and the mouse shows him where he might find berries to help ease his hunger. When the Heavy Boots come close to his hiding place, a swarm of mosquitoes rises and forces them from the swamp. Do the animals know they are helping a runaway slave find the next safe house?

We finally come face to face with Barefoot as he finds a safe haven in a nearby cabin. The interdependence of man with nature is brilliantly cast in this thoughtful story taken from a page in our collective history.

Emberley, Michael *Ruby*

As Ruby heads for Granny's house with some triple-cheese pies in her basket, she is given two warnings by her mother: never trust a cat and don't read as you walk. Ruby is a girl after our own hearts! Of course, she meets a slimy reptile who threatens her, and she is given protection by a somewhat suspect Good Samaritan. This Samaritan, who looks remarkably feline, wants to know where Ruby is going. Ruby is much too astute to be taken in by the wily ways of a stranger.

You will love this alternate telling of the Red Riding Hood story, and you will delight in the comeuppance that is a just reward for the feline intent on having a delightful "mouse"ful for his next meal.

Fleischman, Paul *Weslandia*

Wesley does not fit in with his classmates or his neighbors. The only sport he excels at is running from his tormentors. Then one Wednesday, just as school is about to let out for the summer, Wesley learns that each civilization has its own staple food crop. Now Wesley has a summer project!

Wesley plows a plot of land in his backyard and determines to leave the ground open to chance, to see what will develop. It is amazing to watch as Wesley's staple crop provides all that he needs for his own civilization. You will want to know what happens when Wesley returns to school in September.

Paul Fleischman never ceases to amaze me with his remarkable talent for creating stories and verse that are original and oh, so memorable!

Janeczko, Paul *That Sweet Diamond*

I love baseball. I have some favorite teams and I have been known to stop on a long trip home to watch the Blue Jays play. There is so much to see and so much that is peculiar to this national pastime.

Paul Janeczko also has a soft spot for the sport and is able to translate that love into a series of poems that explores it from many perspectives, on the field and off. His poetry includes the fans, the atmosphere and the players who play the game with raw talent and an enthusiasm that raises the spirit of those of us who call ourselves fans. The poet is able to create visual images second to none through word choice and placement. I will return to this book every spring to share the glory of the game with my students.

King, Thomas *Coyote Sings to the Moon* ❧

We should all be exposed to such original and witty stories as this one. It makes my listeners laugh out loud and serves as an excellent example of a "pourquoi" tale. When Old Woman and the animals come down to the pond to sing to the moon, Coyote asks if he might sing a chorus or two. They are reluctant, and hilarity follows.

Moon is so disturbed by Coyote's voice that she leaves the sky. The animals and Old Woman are left to find her and coax her back. It proves impossible until Coyote becomes involved once more. He finds Moon and offers to bring her back. Old Woman has her own plan, and Coyote is to be the star performer. He does his job too well!

Coyote Sings to the Moon has been a perennial favorite since I first began reading it four years ago. The children never tire of hearing it. One class loved it so much that their teacher created a scripted piece for an assembly performance. Each child had a part to play, and the main characters were chosen with their vocal strengths and comedic skills in mind. The coyote's song resonated through the gym as the audience delighted in the humor of the story. This performance was the hit of the season, and they received many requests for an encore.

Little, Jean *Hey World, Here I Am!* ❦

Shelley Harwayne, a senior superintendent in the New York City school system says that the best thing about this wonderful book is its title! I agree that no other title would fit the tone of the writing or the characters we meet as we read its pages.

You may have met Kate in two previous books by Jean Little. Her poems play a part in the text for *Look Through My Window* and *Kate*. Kate's strength of character is evident, as are her friendships, her loves and her opinions concerning the ways of the world. Kate is not afraid to take a stand or to stick to her principles. She is a writer and uses her writing to make observations and state opinions. She is a person worth knowing, and there is no better way to get to know her than to read this book of Kate's poems.

> *"People who read condensed versions instead of the real book," I said loftily, "are like people who read a road map and think they've been on a journey."*

Major, Kevin *Eh? to Zed* ❦

We are always on the lookout for books that speak of what it is to be truly Canadian. Kevin Major has tapped his creative genius to bring this thoughtful, and very entertaining, alphabet book to life. The illustrations are inspired by Major's comprehensive list of things Canadian. It is a true collaboration of vision and spirit.

No matter how often I go back to it, I am surprised by a new image or thought. The choices made for the twenty-six quartets of rhymed words are explained following his initial text. The inspiration for the artwork is cultural and historical. This is a wonderful souvenir gift for visitors to our land, a treasure to be shared within our families and an exemplary resource for our library shelves.

Mills, Lauren *The Rag Coat*

This book is perfect for reading at the beginning of your year to create a sense of community that values every child who walks through your classroom door. In a poor mining family there is no money for extras. When Papa dies and Minna has no coat, she decides that she will not start school as she will just have to quit when the weather turns. To her rescue come the quilting mothers, who pool their scraps and create a beautiful coat of colors for Minna to wear. She loves it! Imagine her despair when her schoolmates torment her about the rags that went into making it. But Minna has an ace up her sleeve. Her rag coat has many stories to tell, and tell them Minna does.

> Our grade four teacher reads *The Rag Coat* each year on the first day of school. It helps her to establish a sense of caring within her classroom. It provides a perfect platform for discussion concerning the way a community works to help all who live there. It opens the children's eyes to the stories they have to tell, just as their bits of clothing provided stories for Minna to share with them. It is thoughtful and can provide an atmosphere that will enhance the life of the classroom as the children move to become fast friends in the coming days.

San Souci, Robert *The Talking Eggs*

In a classic tale of "you get what you deserve," we meet sweet Blanche and her cross and mean older sister, Rose. Like Cinderella, Blanche is made to do all the work, while Rose and their mother fan themselves lazily on the front porch.

Then Blanche meets and helps an old woman and is blessed by her with good fortune and many riches. Of course, Rose is jealous. She gets her comeuppance when she meets that same old woman and treats her with her usual disdain and disrespect. We are left to sigh with approval over the fates of all three women. Each gets what she so richly deserves.

Van Allsburg, Chris *The Widow's Broom*

Chris Van Allsburg is a master of irony. His stories are flawlessly told, and most end with a perfect twist. In this story, an old woman befriends an injured witch, who disappears, leaving her old broom behind. Minna assumes that the broom has lost its power, but soon it is helping with household chores. When Minna's neighbors discover the broom's power, they are certain that it must be wicked.

When the broom has a run-in with two nasty neighborhood children, it is seized and burned. Thinking that they have solved their problems, the neighbors are skeptical when Minna reports that she has seen the ghost of the broom. I will leave it to you to discover the ironic twist.

Viorst, Judith *Sad Underwear and Other Complications*

There are too many complications in life! What might happen on the first day of school? Who decided that birthdays only come once a year? Why leave out unicorns and give us snakes? How can you ask a princess to clean up the mess that is made when the castle sleeps for one hundred years?

This book of poetry is filled with the angst of childhood and with children's many unanswerable questions. The poems are irreverent and hilarious; kids will quickly pick favorites to read again and again. The rhythm of the language and the careful choice of words make this a delight for the tongue and ear. An ideal companion to *If I Were in Charge of the World*.

Waboose, Jan Bourdeau *SkySisters* ❧

Two young sisters eagerly prepare to venture out into the cold winter night, with their grandmother's words singing in their heads: "Wisdom comes on silent wings." It is so hard to be silent in the beauty of this night. As they stand beneath the starlit sky, they wonder how long they might have to wait. The trek to Coyote Hill is filled with the sights and sounds of their northern home. They see deer and rabbits and hear the coyote's song. As they patiently wait for the SkySpirits to appear, they dance together and make snow angels. Finally, their patience is rewarded and they gaze in silent wonder at the beauty of the northern lights. Lucky are we who have shared this natural wonder.

Wynne-Jones, Tim *On Tumbledown Hill* ❦

It begins with twenty-six words and surefire mischief. As the words diminish page after page, and the artwork begins to fill the space, we realize that the artist has some concerns for his safety. He considers leaving, but fears the monsters will follow. Perhaps he should set his mind to the task at hand and try to ignore their existence. It takes some doing, but as he concentrates on his work, it seems that the monsters disappear. Or do they?

An amazing blend of talent creates this language-rich story and couples it with inventive art and a perfect ending!

Part iv: *Lucie Poulin-Mackey*

As the reader develops, he or she needs to be challenged. Children may be challenged by level of difficulty or by themes in stories or by ideals. At this age, they are old enough to express opinions and make judgments on what they read. They also like to involve themselves in social issues. More than at any other age level, I found it easy to get my eight- to eleven-year-olds involved in activities such as volunteering at the local food bank and organizing fundraisers for the needy. They become less conscious of themselves and their needs and can concentrate on others. I remember teaching my students to knit (yes, even the boys) in math class. Each student was responsible for a square that we then assembled into an afghan and raffled off. The proceeds of the sale went to an African mission. I have provided titles that can provoke discussion, but also tickle the funny bone.

Beauvais, Daniel *Ajurnamat! On n'y peut rien!* ❦

Set in the far north in the Bay of Ungava, this book is full of emotions that will bring you to the edge of your seat. Follow the heroic exploits of a nurse, the only medical officer of the local village, trying desperately to save the life of a young man in need of an operation. Will she be able to get the help she so desperately needs, despite the fierce snowstorm raging outside? A book for the adventurous soul in us all.

Demers, Dominique *La nouvelle maîtresse* ❦

This school day begins differently. The class is silent. The students hear a sloshing sound coming from the hallway. The door opens and a strange-looking skinny lady enters wearing a witch's hat that is rounded at the top. She is the substitute teacher, but she is far from your average teacher. You will fall in love with this endearing character.

And you will want to catch her in her other adventures, *La Mystérieuse Bibliothécaire*, *Une bien curieuse factrice* and *Une drôle de ministre*. Mlle Charlotte is so popular that she is featured in a Richard Ciupka film, *La mystérieuse Mlle C*. I'm willing to bet that the Mlle Charlotte series will create the same phenomenon in French Canada that Harry Potter did worldwide. A must have for your book and DVD collection.

> *Lorsqu'elle lit un roman vraiment passionnant,*
> *mademoiselle Charlotte tombe dans l'histoire.*
> *Son corps reste ici, mais son esprit voyage ailleurs.*

Gingras, Charlotte *La fille de la forêt* ❦

Avril's mother has died recently, so Avril must now leave her mining town, her beloved forest and lakes. She is placed in a foster home in the city. Avril cannot live in these conditions and leaves the home. In the streets she meets up with three other characters. Their meeting turns out to be destiny, for they are to help a stranger whose dream is to plant a forest in the middle of the ghetto. They must fight city hall in order to realize his dream.

Jonas, Anne *Tibert et Romuald*

This is the endearing story of Romuald, a young adventurous mouse confined to the library of the house for fear of Tibert, the gruesome monster. Romuald can't bear his confinement anymore; he must leave his prison no matter the cost. While he is out and about, his fears overcome him and he scrambles to the safety of the bookshelves. A book falls to the ground, and Romuald is stirred by the images he sees in it. When he sniffs it, the book speaks: "You eat me with your eyes." Thus begins Romuald's great adventure.

This book promotes the love of reading by all and the power reading can have for all of us. I highly recommend it.

> *Elle parlait de rivières, de mers, de montagnes,*
> *de forêts et de dragons verts. Et Romuald*
> *comprit ce qu'étaient ces choses qu'il n'avait*
> *jamais vues. Il avait chaud, il avait froid, il*
> *était heureux, il avait peur, il riait. Il sentit*
> *même une petite larme qui roula de ses yeux*
> *et glissa le long d'un poil de ses moustaches.*

Marchildon, Daniel *Le pari des Maple Leafs* ❧

Yes, another hockey story, but I assure you not just your average one. Adventure, intrigue and a few surprises await you in this book. The Maple Leafs are having another of those seasons. They must recruit a new goalie whose presence on the team will create controversy not only for the team, but also for the league and the world of hockey. Professional hockey will never be the same. Do you remember Manon Rayaume? Well you should, because the new goalie for the Leafs in this story is a girl. A great read for all. It might get you to look at hockey in a whole different way. Go, Leafs, go!!!!

> *Vingt et un ans de métier et j'ai jamais*
> *vu ça, une gardienne de but.*

Marcotte, Danielle *La terreur des mers* ❧

As early as 1590, pirates roamed the Caribbean, pillaging and wreaking havoc as they searched for adventure and riches. Follow the story of Dent d'Or (Golden Tooth), son and grandson of pirates, who has survived storms, shipwrecks, treason and other perils. But will his seaman's skills serve him on land? This time it's he who could be the victim. A story of adventure that just might get your boys reading again.

Mativat, Daniel *Le duc de Normandie* ❧

"Since you were born you have conducted yourself like a dog, and so you shall remain until you repair your wrongdoings." Follow the adventures of the Duke of Normandy, proud warrior of the Crusades, retold by an author whose passion for history shows in every page.

Mignot, Andrée-Paule *Lygaya*

This historical adventure is told by a twelve-year-old recalling his family history. On the eve of his hunter initiation, Lygaya has difficulty sleeping. He thinks of the hunt that is ahead of him. Will he be a valiant hunter like his ancestors? Loud noises reach his ears. Soon a stranger brandishing a sword yells that he must come outside. Who are these strangers and what do they want? This is a tale of slavery from Africa to the Americas. Follow the hardships of Jean-Baptiste's ancestors.

Noël, Michel *Le capteur de rêves* ❦

This is an aboriginal tale about the birth of the dream catcher. A spider has made the elders' tent a home for some time. One day she takes a human form and shares with them the secret of the dream catcher. "It is round," she says, "like our grandfather moon and our mother earth. Its powers will catch the bad dreams and its feathers will keep the good ones." A great read that inspires respect for the founding nations of our country.

Nöstlinger, Christine *Le môme en conserve*
Translated from German by Alain Royer

Madame Bortolotti loves to order from catalogues, by phone, by mail. So much does she love her habit that she sometimes forgets what she has ordered. One morning she receives a strange package with a note. "Dear Madame Bortolotti," it says. "We regret the late arrival of your order. Due to unforeseen difficulties with the manufacturer we were unable to deliver your package on time. We hope that everything is satisfactory. You may return the package within the next twenty-four hours in its original unopened packaging." Her memory fails her at times. She doesn't remember ordering a child. Follow the adventures in this humorous tale of instant motherhood.

Oppel, Kenneth *Sylverwing* ✻
French text by Luc Rigoureau

What a coup de force! This young Canadian author has raised the bar with this, the first of the Silverwing trilogy. Through the eyes of the main character, a bat, the reader is captivated with every turn of the page. I was recently in a grade four class in a French first-language school where I found this book in their reading baskets. I was amazed to find such a thick book in their repertoire. One student said that he was not intimidated by the number of pages and was actually on the second book and looking forward to the third. Both girls and boys in the class assured me that it was an excellent read. They were right! Bravo!

Paquette, Denise *Griboullis barbares* ✻

Set in the small New Brunswick town of Grande-Digue, this book tells the tale of a dispute between vacationers and a local who is desperate to save her small piece of land from the devastation of erosion. She meets resistance when she must interfere with people's holidays in the name of the environment. A good read featuring local colors and attitudes of the East Coast.

Pelletier, Maryse *Duo en noir et blanc* ✻

Vincent is discouraged. His rock band is splitting up; his friends seem to be abandoning him; even his best friend, Jackson, is cutting the ties. For his part, Jackson must deal with racial issues. He must establish his identity in the face of the white world that surrounds him. In one summer, Vincent and Jackson must find their way in a world that they think has left them behind. A captivating story of self-discovery and growing up.

Poitras, Anique *Lysita et le château. Miro et le château.* ✻

The neatest concept I've seen in a long time. On one side you read the girl's story and on the other side you read the boy's story. And in the middle they meet. Both Lysita and Miro are afraid of flying. That's a hard pill to swallow when you're a sorcerer's apprentice. Desperate to become valued students, they discover their true vocation through their encounter with Céleste, an accomplished witch.

Soulières, Robert *Le baiser maléfique* ❧

A retelling of a legend first told in the 1700s in a village in the Rimouski region of Quebec. It was said that on the night of Mardi Gras, people should organize festivities and enjoy life to the fullest, but at the stroke of midnight all festivities must end to avoid grave danger. In this story, Rose Latulipe, who loves to dance, asks her family to organize such a feast for her last Mardi Gras at home before she weds her beloved. "Make it so," says her father, "but under the condition that we stop all festivities before Ash Wednesday begins." All is well until eleven p.m., when a tall dark stranger knocks at the door and asks to come in to warm himself. Rose is taken by this stranger who dances so well. Will she defy the taboo or obey her father's warnings?

> *Après avoir observé longuement toutes les jeunes*
> *filles du bal, l'étranger se dirige vers Rose pour*
> *lui demander si elle accepterait de danser avec lui.*

As Literacy Curriculum Leader, I am asked on occasion to visit classrooms and teachers. In one such instance I came across a teacher who in her preparation to read a story out loud to her students left all of us in awe, wanting to have the story read to us. She presented a timeline of religious events found in the Catholic calendar surrounding Easter (Mardi Gras and Ash Wednesday). She presented the definitions of some difficult words and also introduced us to the various characters, giving us some clues to their personalities. Finally, she distributed several roles to different children in the class. I never will forget the way she presented *Le baiser maléfique*. Thank you, Anita.

CHAPTER FIVE

Twelve- to Fourteen-Year-Olds

Part 1: *David Bouchard*

This is the stage when reading is supposed to take off. Children are expected to have become independent readers by this time in their lives. And often they are. Strong readers usually attain this stage sooner in life than this; however, we must not take this age group's ability to read for granted.

Some of our children are not ready to be left to their own devices at the age of twelve. We must continue to hold their hands. We must nurture their love and passion for the written word, particularly now, if they are unable to achieve it on their own.

The entire world is talking about Harry Potter. Every child deserves to be a part of that world. If children are not strong enough readers to read the books themselves, Mom and Dad or someone at school must be there to read them to them, whether they are nine years old or thirteen. We must maintain a high level of involvement. We must maintain their interest in the written word.

At this age it becomes more difficult for weak readers to hide their struggles. We must treat our kids with kid gloves. Keep in mind the theory behind yin and yang: if our children are weak readers, they are surely strong in something else. It is for us to maintain the balance between what we are trying to achieve in reading and the strengths that God has given each child. If a child is strong in athletics, make sports a big part of the child's world and success. If a child is strong in art, then let art play a dominant role in your daily routine.

And finally, take the multisensory approach! Keep in mind the influence the Internet is having on our children. They get it all on-line: text, visuals and sound. They can get it all in books as well. Use whatever means are available to you to capture and hold the interest of all your children. Seek out and use picture books, books on tape or film, plays, toys and games related to books.

For twelve- to fourteen-year-olds who are weaker readers, the work has just begun. Good luck!

Avi *Something Upstairs*

I LOVE so much of what Avi writes, and this is my favorite of his many books. Like many men who share my reading style and interests, I favor non-fiction. If and when I do read fiction, I favor historical fiction. Set in Rhode Island, *Something Upstairs* has it all: a ton of history, a touch of time travel and high-level suspense. When Kenny realizes that his attic room was once inhabited by a slave, he feels compelled to get to the root of his mysterious roommate's murder. Kids love this book — at least they do when I read it to them. And yes, it does matter that the person reading loves what he or she is reading.

> *A white glow, almost shiny, and brightest on the floor, filled the windowless space. And what Kenny saw — or thought he saw — were two hands, then two arms, reaching up from the stain, pushing away a box of his mother's old books that was sitting on it. These hands and arms seemed to be not flesh and blood but sculptured, glowing smoke. It was as if, from under that box, a body was struggling to be free.*

Avi *The Man Who Was Poe*

Rather than apologize for including yet another repeat author, let me speak to the value of getting kids hooked on certain writers. As with other things, it is true that you should keep going back to a good thing once you've found it. If you find that a certain genre of book or a certain author grabs your child or your students, go there again and again. This piece of historical mystery takes us right back to the days of the amazing Edgar Allan Poe. Who was he, really? This book is similar to *Something Upstairs* in that it is founded in history and suspense and is very well written.

Corlett, William *The Steps up the Chimney*

British writer William Corlett's series The Magician's House has been made into a television series that has been aired in North America as well as in Europe. Magic, time travel and a passion for conserving the environment make this series of four books a winner with youth and adults alike. The attic is visited by a wizard, a magician who, with the help of four bright and caring children, shapes events that could drastically alter the house and valley which they all love dearly. I didn't find these books to be the best read alouds; I recommend that you read them on your own — you and your children. Then let the sharing begin.

Dahl, Roald *The Wonderful Story of Henry Sugar and Six More*

Roald Dahl has appeared on one of my lists thus far, and here he is again. This book is a collection of seven short stories that are absolutely captivating. And they are great read alouds. Teachers, make this a big part of your collection. You'll read them to your grade four to eight kids again and again. That is a promise! Parents, don't miss out on the fun. Get this book and read each story aloud with your children.

Heneghan, James *The Grave* ❦

A Liverpool youth falls into a mass grave that dates back to the potato famine in Ireland. He travels back 150 years to meet and develop relationships with his Irish grandparents. Had you asked me last week if I liked time travel books, I would likely have said no. However, seeing that I am recommending yet another, I realize that I do. And this book — my, oh my!

Lawrence, Iain *The Buccaneers* ❦

This is one of a series of three books that follows the adventures of a young man on the high seas. Can you imagine a prairie boy recommending books about pirates? This, I can assure you, will be the only time that I do. Iain Lawrence reeled me in with the first in his series and propelled me through the next two. I honestly can't even recall what prompted me to pick the first one up in the first place. My guess is that these books will be a bigger hit with boys than with girls, but that holds true with much of what appeals to me. One passage will bring out the tissues. I've read it to several people and it has yet to fail me. THAT I like!

Oppel, Kenneth *Silverwing* ❦

In the tradition of E.B. White's charismatic pig, Wilbur, Oppel has created an amazing little bat named Shade, the protagonist in this series of fast-moving adventure novels. One need only read Oppel's first hit, *Silverwing*, to understand the series' success. I can't think of a series other than Harry Potter that our children are talking about more than this one. *Silverwing* is good. *Sunwing* is better and *Firewing* is my favorite of the trilogy (and it is the favorite of many young people I've talked with). Yes, they read well aloud.

Paulsen, Gary *Hatchet*

Hatchet has sold a million copies worldwide. These numbers alone say it all about this story of a teenaged boy left alone in the wilderness with nothing but his wits and a hatchet. Many Gary Paulsen books are perfect for kids of this age. *Harris and Me* is one of my favorite read alouds ever. *Puppies, Dogs and Blue Northers* is one of my favorite books. You've read my thoughts on *Nightjohn* and the Culpepper series. Go ahead, read this one, but don't miss out on Paulsen's many other books.

Richardson, Bill *After Hamelin*

Books that are based on widely known stories often appeal to weaker readers and those who are difficult to hook. Most of us are familiar with the Pied Piper. Here is a creative look at what might have been. Again, if this works for you and your children, there is an entire body of work out there with much the same allure. I've already listed *The Oxford Book of Modern Fairy Tales*, and Donna Jo Napoli and Robin McKinley are two of many writers who create new stories based on popular fairy tales. It is rare that I do not enjoy this type of read, and I very much liked *After Hamelin*.

Rowling, J.K. *Harry Potter and the Philosopher's Stone*
(*Sorcerer's Stone* in U.S.)

I know that most kids in this age group will have seen the movie, read the books or had the books read to them. You will likely have read the entire series aloud to your children or students before. Now is a good time for a full, comprehensive silent read. Harry Potter is that important. Harry Potter deserves that kind of attention.

> Newspapers around the world are excluding Harry Potter from their best-seller lists. This phenomenon has made up the top of every best-seller list in North America for years now. Newspapers add a footnote mentioning that the list excludes Harry Potter books. In spite of this unbelievable success, many adults have yet to read the series. How can this be possible? If the world's children are captivated and clearly in love, how can we, those responsible for and in love with these children, not read what they love? Are we not ourselves literate? How can we sit down at the supper table or walk about on the playground and talk about books and reading with our children when we are not reading what they are reading? There are no excuses. You simply MUST read Harry Potter!

Sachar, Louis *Holes*

Until he wrote *Holes* and won the Newbery, Louis Sachar was best known for his off-the-wall humor. I've had success with his Wayside School series. *Holes* is a wonderful story about a teenage boy stuck in a reform camp where "delinquent" boys are forced to dig holes in the middle of a dry lake bed. The story focuses on the relationships among the boys and on boy-related pressures and problems. As a bonus, this is a superb read aloud.

Spinelli, Jerry *Maniac Magee*

Another Newbery Award winner and another book that boys enjoy. This is a story with mythic elements about a boy who runs away from home to a place where people are divided by race. In subtle ways, Maniac creates bonds between people on both sides and some ties for himself at the same time. While it has great depth, *Maniac Magee* also has a feel of other books about gangs and peer pressure, making it highly accessible.

Spinelli, Jerry *Stargirl*

This is one of only three books that I've been able to get my non-reading agent to read and enjoy. The story line of a young, free-spirited girl living (and falling for a boy) in a typical yuppie community wouldn't normally grab me; however, this one did. *Stargirl* deals with peer relationships and pressure. It is set in a typical high school; in fact, it feels somewhat like Sweet Valley High. For a weaker reading hockey player, you would think that nothing could be less appealing. However, Spinelli has a unique perspective on people and events. This book works! It grabbed hold of me and hung on to the last page.

Tolkien, J.R.R. *The Hobbit*

Next to Harry Potter, this is my favorite series. This book (and the series) appeals to almost everyone. It most certainly does to boys (though my wife Vicki loves it as well). Read it aloud. Read it silently. Listen to it on tape or CD. Watch the movie. Reading really doesn't get any better than this.

> *The Hobbit* and The Lord of the Rings are more difficult to read and understand than is Harry Potter. Harry Potter is set in today's world. Tolkien's world is not of our world. For some, a written description of Middle Earth might suffice. For others, Middle Earth will be better understood if defined visually. When it was time for my youngest son, who inherited many of his father's reading problems, to be introduced to *The Hobbit*, I knew that he would have difficulty reading it. I also knew that he deserved it. I bought him the series on tape. My favorite rendition is that of the BBC's *The Mind's Eye*.

Part II: *Anne Letain*

This list picks up where the last left off, with young people reaching into adulthood and coming to grips with their personal places in the

universe. Tinged with some humor (*The Secret Diary of Adrian Mole,
A Year Down Yonder*), this is by and large a serious list that contains
some formidable writing (*The Golden Compass, Whirligig, Angel's Gate,
The Changeover*), but which will provide a huge return for the effort.
Mostly realistic, there is still much room left for hope and imagination. Although the heroes of these books are largely young people,
there is no reason why adults cannot delve in and relish the scope
and, yes, beauty of these books. If certain children have become fluent
and more sophisticated in their bookwants by this point, this is the list
for them.

Almond, David *Kit's Wilderness*

Dark and difficult, *Kit's Wilderness* explores the realm of magic realism
through the eyes of its young male protagonist (Kit). From the game of
Death that is brutally played out in the first chapter, Kit's personal and
physical wildernesses are explored with tenderness and insight. Inaugural
winner of the American Library Association's Printz Award for the best
in young adult fiction, with *Kit's Wilderness*, David Almond provides
readers with a spine-chilling roller coaster of a novel.

Bloor, Edward *Tangerine*

Paul Fisher, a legally blind seventh grader, moves with his family to
Tangerine, Florida, where he lives in a gated community that is not
exactly the American Dream. Paul is often on the sidelines as his father
pursues his dream of a pro football career for Paul's older brother,
Erik. Still, Paul carries on while a series of mysterious and seemingly
inexplicable events threaten to ruin his life. This is a taut, multithreaded
read that climaxes with a gripping revelation and redemption for
Paul. *Tangerine* could be described as boy athletics successfully wed to
American gothic.

Cooney, Caroline *What Child Is This?*

Three disparate young people find their lives intertwined at Christmas:
Liz, who is almost blessed with too much, and Matt and Katie, two foster children living in the same home. When Katie writes her Christmas

wish for a family on a paper bell hanging in a local restaurant, she sparks a chain of events that eventually leads to a fitting and heartwarming conclusion. As ever, Cooney delivers the adolescent voice and angst. It's great to have a Christmas tale that is appropriate and meaningful for this age group.

Crew, Gary *Angel's Gate*

Eleven-year-old Kim narrates this tale of mystery and intrigue from the Australian outback. The story starts with the murder of Paddy Flanagan, a gold digger living in the rough with his two wild children: teenager Leena and eight-year-old Mickey. Leena is taken into the care of Kim's doctor and nurse parents, while Mickey is still missing. With the murderer at large, it falls to Kim to protect Leena and to find the autistic Mickey. With some parallel side plots, which add to the mounting tension, Crews creates a real page-turner. This is a stunning read, made more effective by Crew's tantalizing use of setting. You'll be dying to go to Oz!

Fine, Anne *The Tulip Touch*

Natalie moves to a new town and school and falls under the spell of Tulip, a psychologically disturbed and damaged local girl. Natalie is pulled further and further into Tulip's world of near evil until she ultimately manages to break off the relationship. Then Tulip wreaks a terrible revenge. Written simply, and accessible to quite young readers, the power of this book lies in the content and the disturbing emotions that linger long after reading it.

> I have workshopped *The Tulip Touch* with a group of nine- and ten-year-old girls. The most fascinating question of the discussion was asked by one of the girls as a round-the-table question and answer. She wanted to know whether each of us would or could have resisted Tulip's evil lure. The answers were illuminating—some of these girls knew in their hearts that they would not have been able to pull away from Tulip. I was surprised that at so young an age these girls were so aware of peer influence and recognized their own helplessness.

Fleischman, Paul *Whirligig*

Brent Bishop, humiliated by a popular girl at a party, drives home drunk and attempts to kill himself. Instead, he kills Brianna, whose grief-stricken mother, in some kind of wish for atonement, sends Brent to the four corners of the United States to erect whirligigs in honor of her daughter, who had so loved them. In doing so, Brent achieves some inner sense of himself. The language of this short book, much like the whirligigs themselves, whirls and soars, and the reader is given permission to examine some of life's universal conundrums.

Garfield, Leon *Smith*

Smith, a twelve-year-old illiterate ragamuffin surviving in Victorian London, empties the pockets of a gentleman and then witnesses his murder. He finds himself in possession of a document that is wanted by others in the London netherworld, and his attempts to save himself are told with speed and vitality. Garfield was a gifted storyteller, and it is wonderful that his books have been recently republished for another generation of readers.

Halvorson, Marilyn *Cowboys Don't Cry* ❦

Shane Morgan's mother has died and his father, an itinerant rodeo clown, begins to drink heavily. When Shane's grandfather dies and leaves them a ranch in the shadow of the Alberta foothills, Shane sees it as an opportunity for school and a regular kind of life. Of course, his new life does not unfold exactly as he would want it to. *Cowboys Don't Cry* is an emotional first-person narrative that makes the reader wish for more. Halvorson has a strong sense of place, which also makes the book appealing.

Lawrence, Iain *Ghost Boy* ❦

In a poignant and strange picaresque novel, Iain Lawrence explores what it means to be different or flawed or misunderstood. Harold, an albino, leaves home when he can no longer endure the never-ending taunts and seeks to go to the one place where he believes he belongs, the traveling circus of the 1950s. The "freaks" Harold encounters teach him a thing or two about acceptance and also drive an unpredictable plot line. This is an outstanding coming-of-age novel.

L'Engle, Madeleine *A Wrinkle in Time*

One of the most studied young adult novels of our times, *A Wrinkle in Time* is worth more than a cursory glance. Meg Murry and her strange young brother, Charles Wallace, try to save their physicist father who is lost in space and time. This is neither science fiction nor strict fantasy, but a novel that is sophisticated in concept and delivery as the Murry children use their intelligence and wits to triumph over evil. Fortunately for us, the Murry family continues the adventure in *A Wind in the Door*, *A Swiftly Tilting Planet* and *Many Waters*.

Mahy, Margaret *The Changeover*

The Changeover is a book that is almost impossible to forget. Using one part magic realism, one part contemporary romance, Mahy weaves together a story full of brooding atmosphere and strong, well-developed characters. Laura Chant lives in a ramshackle single-parent family with her unreliable mother and three-year-old brother, Jacko. When Jacko is stricken with a mysterious illness, only Laura, "a sensitive," can recognize that Jacko is possessed. In her quest to save Jacko, Laura meets Sorenson Carlisle, an older boy and fellow sensitive who may hold the key to Jacko's salvation. This book will be hard to find, but is well worth the search.

Peck, Richard *A Year Down Yonder*

Grandma Dowdel's back and just as feisty and eccentric as ever. This time fifteen-year-old Mary Alice is sent to spend a whole year with her grandmother in downstate Illinois as her parents cope with the Great Depression in Chicago. Mary Alice copes with the challenge of Grandma Dowdel and in doing so proves that the fruit doesn't necessarily fall far from the tree. This book is hilarious and perfect to read aloud. Richard Peck is the consummate storyteller.

"Did your late husband go to war?"

"Only with me," said Grandma,
"and he lost every time."

Pullman, Philip *The Golden Compass*

The first book of the His Dark Materials trilogy, *The Golden Compass* is a tour de force fantasy in which Pullman creates an alternate universe peopled with miraculous creatures, daemons, armored bears and witches. Sinister and demanding, this is Lyra's story as she sets out to seek truth and morality in the world. As we journey with Lyra we experience genuine terror, heartbreak, betrayal and loss and yet are breathless for more at the end. Fortunately, there *is* more in the two equally stunning sequels: *The Subtle Knife* and *The Amber Spyglass*. Not for the faint of heart, but there is something here for readers of all ages.

The Golden Compass was the first novel that I ever attempted as an Oprah-style book discussion with my grade five students. It was really an accident—I was looking for an appropriate title when the remainder book fair was on one spring. They were selling copies of *The Golden Compass* for a dollar. I sold all of them to my good readers and got Scholastic to clean out the warehouse for any extras. So later, when we decided to have a book discussion group, the kids suggested *The Golden Compass* as so many of them had read it. We couldn't stop there and so went on to do *The Subtle Knife*. When I told them that it was too expensive to do *The Amber Spyglass* because the book was not yet available in softcover, baggies full of money started appearing on my desk with little stickies requesting that I order the book. Eventually I ordered twenty hardcover copies for my students so that they could find out what happened next.

Singer, Nicky *Feather Boy*

Nicky Singer's first ever young adult novel is a compelling book about adolescent bullying and its consequences. Told in the first person by Robert Nobel, the victim, *Feather Boy* is a haunting story of triumph and understanding revealed through two intertwined plot lines, one revealing Robert's involvement with Edith Sorrel, a terminally ill senior in a local nursing home. As Robert becomes stronger and stronger,

the reader is pulling with him all the way. This is one very satisfying novel.

Townsend, Sue
The Secret Diary of Adrian Mole, Aged 13¾

Adrian Mole, navel-gazer supreme, first appeared in the early 1980s
and is as fresh as ever. In his diary, Adrian pours out every morsel of
his sorry life: his non-relationship with Pandora, the girl of his dreams;
every zit sprouting on his chin; the chaotic state of his parents' marriage.
Adrian's angst is a laugh-out-loud riot. Thank goodness there are sequels
all the way to Adrian's cappuccino years.

Part III: *Sally Bender*

Until now, I have chosen picture books to fill my lists, and this list does
not waver much from that format. Only two of my choices are novels,
Disconnected and *Torn Away*. We often forget that older and sophisticated
readers still can and do enjoy a well-told story in picture-book form.
We tend to believe that once they can read on their own, they want
longer books and they no longer need someone to read to them. That
is far from the truth. I have led many workshops about great books to
read aloud, and my audience is almost always adult. They love the stories
that I read and often mention the pleasure derived from the listening.
Must it be different for our thirteen-year-olds?

Baylor, Byrd *The Table Where Rich People Sit*

Do you really know how rich your life is? Of course, it depends how
we measure that wealth. Byrd Baylor lives a life filled with the riches of
nature's bounty. Mountain Girl feels that her family is not rich enough;
they sit at an old, scratched-up, homemade table and wear worn-out
shoes. Her parents have another vision of what makes people rich. They
want to see the sky while they work. They enjoy sunsets and having
time to hike the canyons where they live. In the end, it is difficult to
put a price on all those things that add up to leading a rich life.

Bouchard, David *If Sarah Will Take Me* ❦

This remarkable book shows the power of unconditional love and the strength of the human spirit to survive and strive for excellence. The inspiration for writing the story came from a chance meeting between David and Robb Dunfield, the illustrator, when Robb spoke at David's school.

Robb's story is filled with emotion: happiness, love, sadness and inspiration. Robb's art and the poetic verse that David has written to tell Robb's story come from Robb's memories of earlier times when he could walk, move and breathe on his own, which he cannot do now. The two have created a powerful message about the person you can become.

Bunting, Eve *I Am the Mummy Heb-Nefert*

The power of this story comes from its first-person narrative voice, which gives it such presence and impact. Heb-Nefert describes herself as the pampered and beautiful daughter of a monarch in ancient Egypt. One evening she meets the pharaoh's brother, and they fall in love. So begins her life of privilege.

At death, her body is mummified to retain her beauty for her husband for all eternity. When he dies, he lies at her side. And now they lie in a museum where people can peer at them. Viewers are surprised to think they were once people and they whisper their disbelief. Heb-Nefert listens to these conversations and wants viewers to know that she can hear them speak and that she was once beautiful.

Detailed art and precise research heighten the impact of this story for the reader and make it worth more than a glance.

Garland, Sherry *I Never Knew Your Name*

A small boy moves into a neighborhood and notices a young man shooting hoops in the moonlight. He notices that the shooter never plays his game with others, despite his talent. The boy also watches him care for stray dogs, develop a crush on the boy's sister, be teased about his clothes and stay away on prom night.

The boy yearns to make contact with the young man, but never does. When the young man jumps to his death from the roof where he feeds the pigeons, it is left to everyone to try to come to grips with what would cause such a thing to happen, and to the young boy to wish that he been his friend.

Powerful . . . yes. An opening for a discussion about loners and the treatment that they get from those who share their space on this earth.

Heneghan, James *Torn Away* ✤

Declan is thirteen, Irish and bent on revenge. His family has been killed by the British on the streets of Belfast and he is consumed by hatred. Determined to settle the score, Declan cannot be trusted, so he is torn away and sent to live with relatives in Canada. He is not happy with his lot in life and is determined to find a way back to Ireland. But the beauty of his new surroundings and the sympathy of his new family begin to have an effect on him and on his resolve to avenge the wrong done him.

Hrdlitschka, Shelley *Disconnected* ✤

Alex lives on the coast with his abusive father. He makes the decision to run away from the torment and seek a new life in the city. There he is tormented by those who prey upon runaways. Tanner's life, on the other hand, is great. He has terrific parents and a natural ability as a hockey player, but he is plagued by dreams of the sea and by terrible headaches. Chance brings the two boys together, and they soon discover that they have a "connection." This is a page-turner — fast-paced, scary and ultimately satisfying.

Jonas, Ann *Watch William Walk*

Some authors have the most wonderful sense of story. Ann Jonas tells this simple story about a boy, a girl, a duck and a dog with alliterative text. Every word begins with the letter *w*, and she creates an inventive tale of the day's adventures.

It is simple, yet complex. While kindergarteners would enjoy the story, older readers will appreciate the thought and creativity that make this book memorable. Jonas's use of light and shadow adds to the impact of the telling, giving us a bird's-eye view, adding another perspective. Intriguing and filled with surprise, this book is sure to inspire older readers to try their hand at creating something similar. Go to it!!

> The lists grew longer and longer as listeners pondered their ability to create a story using alliterative text. We had just finished reading *Watch William Walk* in a grade seven class when I challenged students to try their hand at something similar. What words could they think of that started with *t*, *d*, *s*, or *l*? Could they use their list to make a sensible short story? Was it harder than they thought? Would working with a willing partner help? What a great way to discover the talent of those who write for children and to wonder at their way with words and imagination.

Macaulay, David *Angelo*

We first meet Angelo as he begins his restoration work on the stucco façade of an old church. It is his job to clean the mess that has been left by years of pigeons perching. As he sweeps the crevices, he notices a small, helpless creature. He scoops it up and takes it home and so begins a friendship that will last throughout their lives.

David Macaulay's detailed and poignant illustrations let us share this enduring friendship. He fills the pages with life . . . the life shared by Angelo and his pampered pet. When she disappears, he returns to his restoration work. He loves it, but he is growing tired. Now it is up to the pigeon to care for her caretaker. In a final tribute, Angelo leaves a lasting legacy that will one day be discovered by others.

Marshall, James *Swine Lake*

James Marshall had a wonderful time writing this twisted tale for the famous ballet. Then Maurice Sendak did his magic with humorous, detailed artwork that extends the story and builds on the humor created in the text. It is a work of collaborative genius!

When the "lean and mangy" wolf finds himself in unfamiliar territory, he is not dismayed. He loves to explore. To his amazement he comes to a marquee announcing a performance of *Swine Lake* by the Boarshoi Ballet. Get it? Filled with wacky wordplay, this is a book for experienced readers and people who appreciate the comeuppance that awaits those who use their wily ways to try to outwit their smaller and weaker counterparts.

McCully, Emily Arnold *The Bobbin Girl*

I have always loved historical fiction. It is a way for me to hang what I want to remember about history on characters and events made real through the talent of skilled writers and artists.

Emily McCully's work often brings to life another era. In this book we meet Rebecca, who is only ten but works all day in a noisy cotton mill. She is happy to be helping her family, but many of her co-workers complain about the conditions. The story is based on the memoirs of mill girls and reminds us of the time in history when women took their place in the workforce and then protested the conditions under which they were forced to work. Standing together gave them a voice. Bravo!

Priceman, Marjorie *My Nine Lives by Clio*

Do you believe that cats have nine lives? You still might find this story hard to believe! It appears at first to be the journal of a cat, Clio, who has lived nine lives all right, each in a different period in history.

Her first entry is penned in the "land between two rivers" (Mesopotamia). She names the constellations while chowing down on fish, crab and crow. Then she moves on to China where she becomes a clock, to Rome where she invents the alphabet, to the rough seas off Iceland, and so on. As we travel with her, we see history in the making.

The journal is original and awe-inspiring. A tongue-in-cheek explanation at the conclusion of the book assures readers of the authenticity of the events described. What a talent!

Rylant, Cynthia *An Angel for Solomon Singer*

Solomon Singer doesn't like his life in a lonely hotel room with no balcony, no fireplace, no pet, no color. He longs for more, so he wanders. After all, he grew up in Indiana, a place famous for wandering. He remembers the fields, the stars and the chirping of crickets.

His wandering leads him to the Westaway Café where he meets a friend, a waiter who serves his food with a smile and an invitation to come back again. Solomon does and begins to find comfort in all that surrounds him.

If you should pass by the Westaway Café, be sure to stop in. You might be lucky enough to see Solomon and meet his friend, Angel.

> *At night he journeyed the streets, wishing they were fields, gazed at lighted windows, wishing they were stars, and listened to the voices of all who passed, wishing for the conversations of crickets.*

Rylant, Cynthia *Soda Jerk*

From its opening in the morning until the door closes on the last customer at night, Maywell's Drugstore is the meeting place for everyone in Cheston, Virginia. Each of the townsfolk shows up there at one time or another. And the soda jerk attends to their needs and hears their chatter. Through his ears, we become acquainted with the people who share his soda fountain counter. We meet old and young, rich and poor, sporty and sedate.

You will come away from the reading of these twenty-eight poems with an affinity for the soda jerk and a realistic glimpse of the people who share his small corner of the world.

Say, Allen *Stranger in the Mirror*

Allen Say quietly tells stories that have a big impact. In this narrative, we are told that Grandpa has gone. We are not told where, but are left to assume that his departure has something to do with his age, for Sam does not want to get old.

When Sam comes down to breakfast the next morning, he has changed dramatically, and others react in disturbing ways to his appearance. No matter what he does, the fact that he seems to have aged affects all who know him. No one recognizes Sam for who he really is. How are we shaped by the perceptions that others have of us?

Shannon, David *How Georgie Radbourn Saved Baseball*

Every April when baseball season opens, fans gather in stadiums and around their television sets to cheer on their favorite teams. But did you know that there was a time when there was no baseball in America? It happened the year that Boss Swaggert hit a terrible slump and was forced from the game he loved. He determined then and there that he would become rich and powerful enough to ban the national pastime.

When he did just that, spring refused to arrive and people faced year after miserable year of icy cold as winter lay upon the land. Leave it to one small boy, born with the spirit of baseball inside, to come to the rescue of baseball fans everywhere. What a great story to start the season in every classroom that boasts baseball fans!

Sis, Peter *Tibet: Through the Red Box*

Oh, that Peter Sis! What a remarkable storyteller he is! In this personal account from his childhood, we learn about the red box that sat just out of reach in his father's study. When his father passed it on to him, he discovered its secret.

Inside was the diary his father had kept while lost in the mountains of Tibet in the 1950s. He had gone there as a filmmaker with a promise to be home in time for Christmas. In fact, a number of Christmases were to pass before he was reunited with his family. Upon his return he shared his unbelievable tales with his son, who was confined to a white bed in a white room. With his father's return came the return of color to Peter's world. Here he shares the stories that his father shared with him . . . a legacy to his own son, Matej.

Smith, Charles R., Jr. *Rimshots*

Charles Smith loves basketball, jazz, hip-hop and photography. That is evident in this compilation of images, poetry and story. Basketball players are not only those who make millions each year in the professional leagues. There is also the kid who lives, breathes and dreams basketball; his court is the driveway in the backyard or the hoops at the school playground. Great players show drive, perseverance and love for the game. In stunning images, both photographic and written, Charles Smith brings the life of the basketball court to the pages of this fine book. The rhythms of the game and the dialogue of the streets where it is played are combined to entice readers to share Smith's work. Team it with his other two books from this fine trilogy, *Tall Tales* and *Short Takes*. What a treat for the ears and the eyes!

Van Allsburg, Chris *The Sweetest Fig*

I have mentioned this talented artist before. I do not want you to forget his name. Your life will be richer for having read his body of work.

When we meet Bibot, the dentist, we recognize him immediately as a man who leaves much to be desired. He has no time for clutter in his life; even his dog is only allowed to bark on Bastille Day. So we are not surprised when he is furious that he has helped an old woman with no money to pay for his services. She offers two figs and a warning about them. I will leave you to imagine what happens when you give direction to a man such as Monsieur Bibot.

Yee, Paul *Ghost Train* ❦

Choon-yi mourns the departure of her father to North America to find work building the railroad. The family is concerned for his safety. When her father sends money, asking her to bring her paint supplies and her artistic talent to record the work, she is delighted and then devastated to find that he has died in an accident.

She works hard to create a lasting portrait of the train engine and the railway, but nothing seems to be just right. Only when she takes a train trip accompanied by the ghostly presence of her father is she able to capture the essence of what cost him and many others their lives. She returns home with her painting and offers it to the winds that will carry home the souls of those whose work brought the railroad to reality.

Yolen, Jane *Encounter*

Stories of Christopher Columbus's first encounter with the people of San Salvador have been written only from his perspective, until now. Jane Yolen envisions what that first meeting must have been like for the Taino people, and she tells the story in the voice of a young native boy. At first fearful, the boy loses his fear when he is enticed by the gifts meant to tame his "uncivilized" tribe. In fact, Columbus and his men were most interested in the gold the Taino people wore and the slaves that they could cart back to Spain.

Imaginative and thought-provoking, this tale gives us an unconventional account of the discovery of America and the fate of the people who first made their home here.

What a conversation got underway when I shared *Encounter* with a group of grade six students. We had been studying explorers and had mostly been reading dry accounts of their voyages and discoveries when I suggested that they might like to hear a fictionalized account of Columbus's discovery of America. At first they were confused by this new version, then appalled by the additional information that Yolen provides following the text. Can it be true that the Taino people no longer exist? What happened to them? Think what independent research might arise from the sharing of this book.

Part iv: *Lucie Poulin-Mackey*

Many young men and women lose interest in reading at a certain age, sometimes because we do not read to them, share our reading experiences with them or give them the opportunity to share their reading experiences with us and with each other. Kids need to be able to talk about books. As adults we do not turn to a friend or a partner and ask if they can hand us a piece of paper because we need to create a new book jacket for the book we've just read. No, as adults we talk about books, we belong to literary circles, we share our reading materials. We have to provide those same experiences for our young readers. Many of these books will spark interest because they are true lived experiences and might get the young reader thinking and sharing.

Agnant, Marie-Céline *Alexis d'Haïti* ❧

Haiti, land of the sun, the sea and the military. Alexis is witness to ravages and exile. On a small frail sailboat he and several others strive to find the land of the free where they hear the buildings hide the sky. Will they make it?

Delaunois, Angèle *La tempête du siècle* ❧

This story is set in one of the worst weather disasters Canada has ever seen, the Montreal ice storm. The book is about experiences of people the author knew and stories that were shared by those who lived them. Find out how one family survived this cataclysmic natural event, what they lived on, what their emotions were and whether they saved their grandfather's cat.

Gravel, François *La piste sauvage* ❧

Given the choice between school and auto racing, Steve Charbonneau would rather race. Steve balks when asked to bring a book to class, but his teacher cuts him off at the pass and offers him a guide on automobiles from the school library. In no time the young man's life is transformed. What will Steve choose, illegal car races or school?

Laberge, Marc *Le glacier* ❧

In this collection of adventures set in the great mountains of the American west, the author follows the trail of the famous climber John Muir. Storms and rain and insurmountable passages are the backdrop to the ultimate challenge between man and nature. Read about one man's will to conquer the insurmountable in his search to realize his vision of the universe.

Marineau, Michèle *Rouge poison* ❧

In Mont-Royal, Montreal, two friends, Sabine and Xavier, find themselves involved in what appears to be a serial murder plot. It seems like a game in the beginning, but soon becomes much more. Sabine's father is the detective heading the case. What will happen when he finds out his daughter is playing detective? Who will solve the case first?

Mativat, Daniel *Siegfried ou l'or maudit des dieux* ❧

In the Viking era, a young blacksmith learns that he is a prince guardian of a magnificent treasure. Magic, love, courage and heroism abound; a captivating read to the very end.

McClintock, Norah *Fausse identité*

French text by Claudine Vivier

It all starts when a picture is published in the local paper and Zanny is swamped with attention. How will she ever find her real father? A thriller at its best, this work received the Arthur Ellis Award for best police novel for youth in its English version.

Noël, Michel *Le cœur sur la braise* ✹

Having had enough of the city and school, Nipishish returns to his village to pursue the fight his father began years ago. He finds his ancestral voice that will make him proud and free. The writing helps us to understand life on a reserve, the heritage and the challenges such a life can create. A tale of ecology, nature and strong traditions.

Poudrier, Élyse *Des vacances à temps partiel* ✹

Anouk is stuck baby-sitting for the summer again. It's a job, but not much fun when you don't get along with your charge, whose only goal in life is to break every swimming record at the local pool. Lucky for Anouk, she can read during his lessons. Will she change her attitude toward the boy when he is barred from the pool for the summer? A story about change and friendship.

Raimbault, Alain *Herménégilde l'Acadien* ✹

The year is 1775 and English soldiers are pillaging a small Acadian village. Herménégilde escapes and seeks refuge with the Micmacs. A story of friendship, culture and history. The main character searches for his family and learns about himself and about the strength of tradition. This is a story for those who wish to learn about the history of two great nations of our country.

Simard, Benjamin *Ben* ✹

You may wonder why I chose another true story for this list. Watching my husband read non-fiction all the time, I've come to understand the male reader a little bit better. If true-life accounts help our young men read, bring them on! This book is set in the great Canadian wilderness and combines the stories of a real woodsman and a young adolescent boy who is called by the immense wild territory of Laurentian Park. A story of personal struggle and self-actualization.

Soulières, Robert *Un cadavre de classe* ✤

A math teacher who was universally disliked is mysteriously killed. The inspectors have many clues, but may not have enough to solve this case. This is a cute story that will have the reader involved from page one.

Tolkien, J.R.R. *Le Seigneur des anneaux :*
Tome 1, La communauté de l'anneau
French text by F. Ledoux

Hobbits, men, wizards, dwarfs and elves and that famous ring that permits its owner to become invisible and gives him unlimited power over others. But at what cost? Well, I think you know the rest. If you are interested in reading this wonderful book in another language, this is the book for you. The descriptions are powerful and enhance the imagination. A classic in any language.

> I was very moved by listening to David (yes, this David) at one of his conferences. He spoke about The Lord of the Rings and how he had hooked his son into reading the book by listening to it on tape. Ever since, I have played books on tape for my children in the car when we have traveled. We love it.

Vacher, André *Entre chiens et loups* ✤

This is a collection of six stories about people and their relationship with the wild. Learn of a special bond between a trapper and his dogs. Read the story of an old man who clears his debt with a wolf. These true stories will capture your attention to the very end and leave you wondering. Set mostly in the Yukon and the Northwest Territories, they take the reader on a voyage of cunning and survival. You can also read another of the author's great adventures in *Alerte à l'ours*.

Vachon, Hélène *Le piège de l'ombre* ✤

Juliette is a typical high school student. She lives with her dad and has a fascination with antique shops. One day she finds herself leaving a shop with a book she has not paid for. She has never done such a thing before. What could have possessed her? She must return the book without being discovered. Will she succeed?

CHAPTER SIX

Fifteen and Up

Part 1: *David Bouchard*

Now it gets tricky. As with my first list, this one is all over the map.

Let me start by reminding readers that much of what is important in this lies in the need for you to develop a deep and sincere pleasure in reading. Your children or your students must see you reading because you love it.

We are all different as readers. I represent a world of reluctant and weaker readers, those who would prefer to do almost anything rather than read. (This is not me today, but it was when I was a child.) What happens to these children like me when they grow up? What books, if any, might they come to enjoy as adults?

My list will not look anything like those of my colleagues. My three friends are strong, avid readers. The books they recommend will reflect who they are as readers. My list reflects who I am. If you are not a big reader or if your reading consists primarily of lighter material, you might find my suggestions of value. Keep in mind that you cannot, nor do you want to try to, deceive your children or your students. You do not want to try to have them believe that you are enjoying something that you are not. Children won't be fooled. The NBA should have based its literacy campaign on honesty, as should you. Seek out material that you sincerely enjoy, and enjoy it with and around your children or students.

And before you write off my suggestion that there is room in your personal library for Time-Life books, consider this. There is absolutely nothing wrong with light reading. The world devours newspapers and magazines. And there is nothing wrong with a child loving to read comic books; Stephen Krashen, in *The Power of Reading*, argues that comics are linguistically appropriate, are not detrimental to reading development and are conduits to book reading. What happens to the child who grows up loving light, easy reading? Time–Life, among others, understands that millions of adult readers enjoy non-fiction presented in an appealing package. If you are that kind of reader (who often seems to be a man), go there. Allow your children or students to see you reading and enjoying exactly what you love to read. It matters less what you are reading than that you are reading and enjoying it.

And do not abandon poetry or picture books, ever. Surround yourself with a variety of print-rich material, making certain that it has been handpicked by you because it is part of your collection and you like it!

Archer, Jeffrey *A Twist in the Tale*

Light reading and short stories are the cornerstone for many reluctant readers. They appeal to many who do not have the time, or who think they don't have the time, to get into a long novel. Jeffrey Archer is one of Britain's most popular writers. *A Twist in the Tale* appeals to me because the stories are short, captivating and each one ends in a unique, unexpected twist. The content is somewhat mature, as are so many of today's high school students.

Dahl, Roald *The Vicar of Nibbleswicke*

Dahl donated part of the proceeds of this short, hilarious book to the Dyslexic Foundation of London. I can only venture to guess at the number of undiagnosed children who are either in or have graduated from our school systems. We are better at identifying and supporting children today than we were even a decade ago; however, cracks remain. This tiny book is perfect for any child or adult who might fit that description. I was one of those children and *The Vicar of Nibbleswicke* worked for me. The hilarious story of a dyslexic preacher who ends up at the pulpit of his hometown church is beyond clever. I've left this book until now as it is somewhat mature in language. Though it is not on this list, *The Gift of Dyslexia* is a great read for anyone whose child is or might be dyslexic.

Dawson, A.J. *Finn, the Wolfhound*

Books that relate to the individual passions of their readers are usually winners. I include *Finn, the Wolfhound* on my list because I am a dog person and yes, I have a large Irish wolfhound. One out of every two North Americans is right there next to me, loving their pets. For you dog lovers, *Finn* is a guaranteed winner. It is the touching and powerful story of an Irish wolfhound lost in the Australian outback. Can you imagine how such a gentle but grand creature might cope with the elements and the wildlife on a continent so far from home?

Not long ago, I was walking my dog, Hagrid, in a local park in Victoria, B.C., when I was approached by a woman unknown to me. She had recognized Hagrid's breed. She asked me if I had read *Finn, the Wolfhound* by A.J. Dawson. I told her that I had not heard of the book or the author. She was shocked, though I couldn't understand why since the book was published in Britain in 1906. The woman insisted that I seek it out and advised me to have a goodly supply of tissues available when I read it. I did as I always do when looking for a book that is possibly out of print. I went home to our library, sat down at the computer and keyed *Finn, the Wolfhound* into www.abe.com. I was immediately linked to dozens of booksellers around the world. Technology has made accessible books that otherwise would not be. Within days, Vicki and I were sobbing over this wonderful book . . . and that was after having read only the introduction.

Dickens, Charles. Edited by Walter Allen *The Short Stories*

Children and adults alike deserve to know the classics. If you are not a strong reader, then you might care to seek out some plays and short stories written by the masters (some plays are easier to absorb than lengthy novels). I find Dickens' short stories readable and moving.

Ferguson, Will *Why I Hate Canadians* ❧

We Canadians have a unique way of laughing at ourselves. *Why I Hate Canadians*, like a few others on this list, is the kind of book that you can leave in the bathroom, in the car or in any location where it might be picked up and leafed through at will. This is a light, fun book that has no direction whatsoever other than to speak to who we Canadians are. This may never become a classic, but it is almost certain to make you smile.

Hemingway, Ernest *The Old Man and the Sea*

Hemingway's tale of an old fisherman's love for and desire to conquer the sea is another classic that worked for me. For those who travel or who are seeking a different approach, get this one on tape, read by Charlton Heston. That done, seek out the movie featuring Anthony Quinn. Both are superb!

Johnson, E. Pauline *Legends of Vancouver* ❧

This is a grouping of short stories based on legends that were told to Pauline Johnson by First Nations elders. A book featuring short, historical, Canadian stories is a sure winner. This book has it all. Pauline Johnson was an eastern Canadian of Mohawk descent. She wrote about the western Canada that she grew to love. Her heritage and interests lay in the history of our First Nations peoples. How can all Canadians not own this book?

Kinsella, W.P. *Dance Me Outside* ❧

Kinsella offends some by the context and use of language with which he writes. He writes humorous fiction about Cree people on their home reserves in central Alberta. If you are able to appreciate the basic elements of respect among all peoples in Canada, *Dance Me Outside* is a light read that you might enjoy. And if this book works for you, Kinsella has several others in the same genre.

Masson, Jeffrey Moussaieff *When Elephants Weep*

Many readers of all ages prefer non-fiction to fiction. Children who grow up preferring non-fiction are likely to become adults who prefer non-fiction. Couple this likelihood with the pleasure that so many readers find in books about animals — and Masson gives numerous examples that seem to prove that animals, like humans, have feelings — and you will see why *When Elephants Weep* was on the *New York Times* best-seller list for what seemed to be forever.

McKinley, Robin *Beauty*

I love books with roots in fairy tales. I enjoy them with the very young and I enjoy them when they have been written for older readers. *Beauty* is a clever takeoff on Beauty and the Beast. There are many such books on the market and this is one of my favorites. Donna Jo Napoli has also written several books in this genre. I've enjoyed many of her books as well.

Rutherfurd, Edward *London*

London is Rutherfurd's sequel to *Sarum*. If you enjoy these, read his book *The Forest*. When you consider that most of my list focuses on short stories, non-fiction and light reading, this book might seem to be a step in the opposite direction. *London* is a long and intense fictional look at the history of England's most important city. Rutherfurd paints an amazing picture of the grand old city while following several families through centuries. What makes his books unique and workable for readers who are as difficult to please as I am is his off-the-wall style. He moves freely among times and locations, taking the reader here and there, not unlike the way we are thrown about while watching television. North American youths are accustomed to being flung from one scene to another, and this is exactly what will make this book appealing.

Shelley, Mary *Frankenstein*

Frankenstein is another classic that hardly needs describing. We all know the story, if not from books then perhaps through comic books or movies. There comes a time in each of our lives when we should get the story firsthand. That time is now.

Stewart, Hilary (Annotator/illustrator)
The Adventures and Sufferings of John R. Jewitt ✤

This book is the ultimate in non-fiction. John Jewitt was captured by the Nuu-chah-nulth people in 1803. After spending over two years in captivity, he escaped. His autobiography was published shortly afterward and has been in print ever since. Jewitt's story might not be considered a classic in the formal sense of the word; however, for well over a century it has captured the interest of many readers of my ilk.

> From the moment that I first found this amazing book until I was done reading it, I was riveted. After finishing it, I told everyone I knew about the life experiences of this unfortunate Englishman who had been held prisoner by one of Canada's First Nations. I talked about Jewitt's journal. I dreamt about it. I wanted to write of my own exciting life experiences, however these existed only in my mind. So I went straight there . . . to my mind. I created my own John Jewitt. I named him Etienne Mercier and I sent him on a whirlwind tour of the Queen Charlotte Islands. The year was 1853.

Time-Life *The Old West* or *The Canadians* series

Now I tread on shaky ground. Has anyone ever recommended books quite as commercial as these? Can you imagine my recommending comic books to your children? I can and I do. Light reading is how most of us learn to love reading. Light reading is a place that we want to take young readers. It is also a place that we want to take parents and teachers who have yet to discover the world of something more. Even if they always stay right there, they are modeling good reading practices and they are reading for the right reason — for the love of reading what interests them.

Tolkien, J.R.R. *The Lord of the Rings* series

This series is difficult for reluctant readers. Unlike Harry Potter, which has its foundations in the real world that we all know, The Lord of the Rings is set in Middle Earth and includes characters and situations that are foreign to its readers. All elementary school-aged children deserve to read Harry Potter or have it read to them, and senior school students deserve to come to know the world of *The Hobbit* and The Lord of the Rings. With technology being what it is today, students might hear it on CD or tape or perhaps watch the movies; however, none should be denied the world of J.R.R. Tolkien.

Whitman, Walt *Leaves of Grass*

Next to Henry Longfellow, Walt Whitman is my favorite poet. *Leaves of Grass* is his most popular collection of poems. This is one of many books of poetry that you should own. If you have yet to discover why, get yourself a copy. Read it again and again. Be sure that you are reading it aloud. You will eventually fall in love with his poems as so many have before you, as I have. Fall in love, then share that love with those you love.

Is this then a touch? Quivering me to a new identity,
Flames and ether making a rush for my veins,
Treacherous tip of me reaching and crowding to help them,
My flesh and blood playing out lightning
to strike what is hardly different from myself . . .

Part II: *Anne Letain*

This final list by age is truly a culmination of the "search for self" that is likely the preeminent theme in books written for the older teen. This journey into personal wilderness and self-examination is most usually explored through the protagonist's contact with the biggies—sexuality, gender issues, death, divorce. The titles selected represent some of the best work by writers in Canada, Australia, New Zealand, Great Britain and the United States portraying the teen as he or she comes of age.

Unfortunately, not many books written specifically for this age group fall far from the tree of realistic fiction—more humor and fantasy would leaven the seriousness of much of what is being currently produced for teens. If we can sustain boys into teenage reading, it's likely time for our authors to come to the table with more high fantasy, continually sought by young males.

Bedard, Michael *Redwork* 🍁

In the same territory claimed by *Skellig* and *Kit's Wilderness*, *Redwork* seems to straddle the divide between fantasy and realism. Cass and his mother, Allison, are forced to take accommodation in a ramshackle house occupied on the main floor by a sinister landlord, Mr. Magnus. Cass takes a job as an usher in a run-down local movie theatre and finds the beginning of romance with Maddie. Together, Cass and Maddie seek to find out the secret of Mr. Magnus and his obsession with alchemy. *Redwork* is one of the best YA novels around to explore the relationship between the young and the elderly.

> I was a teacher-librarian in Fort McMurray, Alberta, when *Redwork* was published, and I remember reading it over the Christmas holidays at my sister's house in Edmonton. When I got back to McMurray, I gave it to a colleague to share with his class as a read aloud because I thought it was so strong. Later, by chance, it was included as part of the spring book fair (junior high), and the kids were so excited to see it. I don't think that I've ever had to make so many reorders for another book anytime since. It's always exciting when you see kids taken up with a book that is as difficult and intense as *Redwork*. This, of course, was pre-Harry!

Book, Rick *Necking with Louise* ✹

Many young adult books are presented from the point of view of the adolescent female. This one is for the boys. It's 1965 and Eric is sixteen, stretching into adulthood and away from his parents. These seven inter-connected short stories chronicle the pivotal years of an indelibly prairie boy. They are fresh and vivid and full of humor. Whether Eric is discovering first love or in great danger in a sudden prairie blizzard or suffering through an interminable summer job, the reader is privileged to share in his life as well as a rich and rewarding narrative.

> I had finished reading *Necking with Louise* and was really impressed with the book, especially the completeness of each story. I sent an e-mail to Dave Jenkinson at the University of Manitoba to share my impressions because he too really liked the book. I mentioned that these stories needed to be recorded for CBC Radio—they had just the right feel. Imagine my surprise when, out of nowhere, I received a demo CD from Rick Book on which he read two of the stories. Little did I know that his real job is in radio and I wasn't the only one who thought the stories should be broadcast! Incidentally, it was a beautiful reading.

Brooks, Kevin *Lucas: A Story of Love and Hate*

Lucas is the universal story of what happens when a stranger arrives in a particular place (in this case an isolated island) and becomes a scape-goat for the locals. Yet Lucas the stranger is also a figure of empowerment and causes Cait, the young narrator, to examine some huge moral dilemmas and to make some life-altering decisions. On another level, *Lucas* is an unusual and moving love story. This is a powerful book that will be well regarded by readers and prize givers alike.

Brooks, Martha *Two Moons in August* ❀

Although *Two Moons in August* is most frequently tucked away on the bookshelf that holds the books on teen grief, the overwhelming aura of this book is that of hot romantic midsummer love. Brooks masters the complexities of character and setting with deep sensitivity. Sidonie and her family are recovering from the recent death of her mother when a young stranger (Kieran) arrives to work at the TB sanatorium where she lives in the medical officer's housing with her father. The ensuing relationship with Kieran is played out with celebration, hesitancy and mystery while the hot prairie landscape almost takes on the dimension of a character. This one's a must for all young women and for anyone who cannot forget the confusion and compulsion of first love.

Burgess, Melvin *Junk*

Junk is a difficult, uncomfortable book that is eminently readable and almost impossible to put down no matter how squeamish the reader feels. This is the story of two ordinary young people, Tar and Gemma, who become trapped in a love affair with heroin. Their story is told through the eyes of the various people who become implicated in Tar and Gemma's lives. The resolution is believable and relatively hopeful, but most certainly not happily ever after. Winner of both the Carnegie Medal and the Guardian Fiction Award.

> *"Someone ought to give parents lessons before they allow them to breed."*

Crew, Gary *Strange Objects*

Original in every sense of the word, *Strange Objects* defies branding by gender. In this spellbinding tale, Crew effortlessly plays out two separate story lines, one from the past and one in the present. The two stories are uncannily linked by a missing ring and a mummified hand. Set in the wilds of Western Australia, this is a unique and complex mystery that is a demanding read and which offers up more than a few riddles for the reader. A well-deserved winner of the Australian Book of the Year Award in 1991.

Crutcher, Chris *Athletic Shorts*

This is a sports book for thinking young adults. It features six tense, exciting stories and some of Crutcher's best-loved characters from other books including *Stotan!*, *Running Loose* and *The Crazy Horse Electric Game*. Although the world of athletics provides the context for each story, the stories are mostly about growing up and facing life's realities: bigotry, AIDS, love, sexual orientation. The bonus is that the reader can prolong the pleasure by delving into the books that star the protagonists of these stories. Humorous and engaging.

Doherty, Berlie *Dear Nobody*

This is THE teen pregnancy book that every young person needs to read. Told in Doherty's lovely and sensitive prose, it is the story of Helen and Chris as they cope with an unexpected and unwanted pregnancy just prior to setting off for college. Told from Helen's perspective in the form of letters to her unborn baby (Dear Nobody) and in Chris's anguished responses to Helen's decision to exclude him from plans for his unborn child, the story is compelling and honest with no neat solutions. Both the characters and the situation are utterly believable.

Edgerton, Clyde *Raney*

In this joyful look at the first two years, two months and two days of a present-day southern marriage, Clyde Edgerton has created a minor modern classic and an absolutely endearing character in Raney, the young bride. Raney, a down-home southern Baptist girl, and Charles, a left-wing liberal, manage to accommodate and thrive despite their hugely different outlooks and families. You can't help but root for both of them as they suffer the slings and arrows of the absurdities they encounter. This one is for everybody, especially readers who love to laugh out loud.

Holubitsky, Katherine *Alone at Ninety Foot* ❦

Not just another contemporary teenage dysfunctional family novel, *Alone at Ninety Foot* is a sensitive portrayal of a young woman coming to terms with the why of her mother's suicide and the changes that terrible event has evoked in her world. Notwithstanding the grim foundation of this story, our young protagonist demonstrates a wide range of emotions including humor. Winner of a number of awards in Canada including the Canadian Library Association (CLA) Young Adult Book of the Year.

Mahy, Margaret *The Catalogue of the Universe*

One of Mahy's earlier and most splendid works, *The Catalogue of the Universe* is another variation on adolescent love and search for self. Angela and her friend Tycho are both imprisoned in particular romantic notions. Angela is obsessed with her unknown father, and Tycho (brilliant, short and homely) is obsessed with the sensual Angela. Through their personal turmoil, both come to some understanding of their place in the universe. As with all of Mahy's best work, the tone is charged with electricity and the story is peopled with unusual characters. The New Zealand setting is also appealing. A challenging and rewarding read.

Major, Kevin *Far from Shore* ❦

Far from Shore is another coming-of-age novel, but this time the setting is Newfoundland. Chris Slade is fifteen years old and grasping for direction in a family pulled down by chronic unemployment. However, Chris rises to life's challenges with humor and an easygoing attitude. Kevin Major is one of those adults who has never forgotten what it feels like to be a teenager, and he creates a believable and appealing character in Chris. He also has a penchant and ear for authentic dialogue and language, which makes this book a treat to read.

Marchetta, Melina *Looking for Alibrandi*

Josephine's life, which until high school had never been complicated by a male presence, is suddenly full of men. Her biological father returns and she attracts the interest of two very different boys from her Catholic high school. Set in the Italian-Australian community of Sydney, this is a vibrant take on what it means to grow up in today's world. Marchetta is a young teacher in Australia and this was her first book. It won immediate acclaim and is featured as part of the Australian senior year English curriculum.

Strachan, Ian *The Boy in the Bubble*

Adam and Anne are star-crossed lovers with no hope for a real relationship because Adam has SCID (severe combined immunodeficiency disease) and has been confined to a "bubble" for all of his life. Anne agrees to become Adam's "life-taster," resulting in serious and unforeseen consequences. Yet Strachan, with insight and, yes, humor, makes this love story between two people who cannot even touch each other both convincing and totally acceptable.

Thomas, Rob *Rats Saw God*

Steve York is in danger of failing high school despite exceptional scores on his SATs and despite being a National Merit finalist. The school counselor gives Steve one last chance to make up his missing English credit. Steve writes this chronicle of his junior year. Steve's parents are divorced, and he has always lived in the shadow of his perfect astronaut dad. Now living with his mom in San Diego, Steve has cathartic and hilarious insight into what went wrong in his family. Thomas has a strong, authentic and wildly funny voice and this book could not have been more hip or cool or funny (especially a first-time sex scene!).

Part III: *Sally Bender*

In this list I have tried to mention as many of my favorite authors as possible. I hope to encourage you to look for other books by these authors. That is what happened to me. My life is enriched by the brilliant writing of these talented people and I continue to read and share their work every chance I get. They write with passion and generosity, believing that young people deserve the very best that they can create. What a blessing to us!

Bell, William *Stones* ✺

What a great writer William Bell is! I have enjoyed each of his novels for different reasons. After setting an earlier novel in small-town Ontario, Bell longed to return to that familiar place. He chose the African Methodist Church, which actually exists, as the location for much of the action for his story.

There, Garnet Havelock spends a night during a nasty blizzard. He is plagued by mysterious voices, haunting and frightful. He hears words that he does not understand, and it takes some time before he is able to decipher them. With the help of Raphaella, a transfer student, he is able to unravel the events that led to a horrifying chapter in his town's history.

Boyd, David *Looking for a Hero* ✺

This is an interesting and well-constructed story. I was intrigued from the beginning by this twisting, turning murder mystery that is not resolved until the final case file is read.

Nicholas is accused of killing Robert Player, a famous rock star. Player was a hero to Nicholas's brother, Christian. Through a series of taped conversations, reports and letters we come to know Nicholas and the people in his life. And in a string of vignettes that accompany the reports we learn the awful truth that led to Nick's arrest. We are left with a question. Is there a hero?

Brooks, Martha *True Confessions of a Heartless Girl* ✺

I had great difficulty putting this book down. Were it not for my desperate need for sleep, I might not have done so. A story about the redeeming power of love, its cast of characters lives on in your heart when the reading is done. The catalyst for the events is the arrival of a young stranger in a small prairie town. She appears suddenly in an old truck she has stolen from her latest boyfriend and brings with her all the pain one heart can hold. Noreen Stall is a heartless girl who wreaks havoc on the protected members of this close-knit community. We become observers of the ways in which love can transform lives and build bridges, and fans of a writer who creates such beautiful and genuine people.

Cole, Brock *The Goats*

I first read this book fifteen years ago and remember it as if it were yesterday. With intensity and impact, Brock Cole constructs a fine story about unforgettable characters.

Howie and Laura are two young teens who are made the butt of an insensitive practical joke while at summer camp. They are marooned without clothing on a deserted island and left to fend for themselves. Humiliated by the situation, they refuse to return to camp until Parents' Day. In the meantime, they prove their mettle with careful planning and independence. The conclusion is optimistic. The two have found freedom in their shared survival. Maturity and self-reliance are important themes in this story for young adults. Brock Cole has painted a world that they will recognize.

Cormier, Robert *The Rag and Bone Shop*

This is Robert Cormier's final novel and proof positive that he had no intention of turning away from the tough topics he chose for his young adult audience. Jason is twelve, quiet and shy, preferring the company of children younger than him. When his friend's sister is found murdered, Jason is eager to tell all that he knows as he was one of the last to see her. Needing a quick solution to a shocking crime, the police bring in Trent, who has great skill as an interrogator.

In a small, hot, windowless room, he plies his skills with Jason, and the reader becomes embroiled in a back-and-forth struggle to see reason in the case. Sad and suspenseful, this is writing that left me feeling stunned at its powerful conclusion. It is partly mystery and partly cautionary tale and not to be missed.

Crutcher, Chris *whale talk*

Leave it to Chris Crutcher to create another athletic hero. Tao Jones is not just your ordinary jock. He is irreverent, with a flair for the sarcastic, and he has no desire to be the "star" that he could be. Instead he assembles a motley crew of swimmers to join him on the varsity swim team. He does not look to the mainstream for his team members. In fact, he sets on its ear everyone's definition of an athlete.

His goal for them is to earn a varsity letter. In their workouts and on bus trips, these young athletes reveal who they are and what they want to be. As readers, we realize that the imperfections in each of us make us human, misfit or not.

> *"Mr. Simet, my English and journalism teacher, says the best way to write a story, be it fact or fiction, is to believe aliens will find it someday and make a movie, and you don't want them making Ishtar."*

Curtis, Christopher Paul *Bud, Not Buddy*

Bud is in a home for orphans. Sent to a foster placement that is anything but homelike, he determines to search for his father. He has with him a suitcase that holds his own secret things and the personal mementos he has from his mother, who died at twenty-six. Included is a poster for a band that he thinks must include his father.

He sets out on the road to Grand Rapids and is picked up by Lefty Lewis. Lefty knows the club where the band plays and takes Bud there, where Bud learns the truth, though it is not what he expects. In a hopeful ending, Bud has a new family and a happy future. Heartwarming and humorous, this story was inspired by a conversation heard at a family reunion about Curtis's grandfather, who once played in a band.

Ellis, Deborah *The Breadwinner* ❧

As I was reading this book, I received an e-mail asking me to sign a petition denouncing the ruling government of Afghanistan for its treatment of women.

This powerful story will bring home to many the deplorable and chilling conditions that have been the lot in life for women living under an oppressive regime. Parvana is a young Afghan girl who lives with her family in poverty under Taliban rule. When her father is imprisoned for unknown reasons, Parvana is forced to take action in order to support her family. She does so with tenacity. We are left with the knowledge that there is much work to be done and many willing to do it. It is a hopeful promise.

This is realistic writing filled with tension and scary in its authenticity.

Hesse, Karen *Out of the Dust*

This gripping story is about Billie Jo and her dad, set in the Oklahoma dust bowl following the death of Billie Jo's pregnant mother in a fire. Dust permeates every pore as Hesse tells her gritty family tale in a series of narrative poems. The text is as spare as the surroundings, but the words are perfect.

Journal entries are dated over a period of two years, taking the reader through seasons that seem never to change as the people wait for life-giving rain. While struggling with adversity and isolated by the grim reality of the dust bowl, Billie Jo remains a strong female character who finally learns that there really is no place like home. Only then can she begin to forgive her father and herself for the sadness that has befallen them.

Johnston, Julie *In Spite of Killer Bees* ❦

Rich in tone and detail, this is Aggie's story. She is the youngest of three sisters and the only one with an uncompromising belief that her mother will return to the family after a long absence. Aggie is right. Mom does return when she hears that her daughters have inherited a house from their paternal grandfather along with his accumulated wealth. Aggie is not suspicious, but her sisters are. While the text has a wacky side, it also has a sensitive concern for the relationships that exist between family members. Here are three young girls trying to find their place in the world, facing a crisis each in her own unique way. We are keen observers of life as they experience it. The solution is satisfying, if not happy.

Jordan, Sherryl *The Raging Quiet*

This is a story of love and hope set in medieval times. Prejudice and ignorance also rear their ugly heads. The wonderful characters hold our attention and claim our hearts. Marnie is independent and feisty, strong and compassionate, and always honest. Raven is in a rage against the world because he lives in silence and is treated abominably by the townsfolk, who suspect that he is the devil's child — or, at least, possessed. He is cut off from the world by his deafness and experiences physical and brutal separation at every turn.

When Marnie befriends him, her motives are suspect and she is eventually tried as a witch by people who live in fear of what they do not understand. *The Raging Quiet* is a magnificent story about ageless and lasting love.

> The first conversations that David and I had focused on books, of course. We were delighted to discover a mutual love of the books that would impact the children in our worlds. And we recommended our favorite authors and titles back and forth, again and again.
>
> One of the first books that I told him about was *The Raging Quiet* . . . luckily! He and Vicki loved it and cried over it. He sent me e-mails talking about its impact on them. Marnie and Raven became real people to us, characters who would pop up in conversations and who helped us see the world in a new and different way. Such is the impact of a great story.
>
> And we discovered that we could count on each other for new suggestions and ideas when selecting books to read. Some of the other suggested titles have not been so successful, but we often agree. It is a blessed thing to have friends who share a love of literature that seems, at times, obsessive.

Lowry, Lois *The Giver*

This is a challenging read and somewhat disconcerting. But it is worth every minute you spend with its cast of characters. In a future world, Jonas awaits The Ceremony of the Twelve, where he will be assigned a career. The setting seems idyllic — no fighting, no racial hatred, only peace and harmony. Jonas is given a special assignment. He is to be The Receiver; he will work with The Giver, a community elder who has the power to teach memory and collective history. They will see beyond the insular life the community leads. But the perfect world comes apart as Jonas faces the delight and dilemma of choice and when he learns a terrible secret about his father and the way that their society works.

Mazer, Harry (Editor) *Twelve Shots*

I read these stories prior to the Columbine tragedy and found myself returning to them in the aftermath. Harry Mazer has collected writing from some of today's finest writers. Each story has, at its heart, a gun. Funny, poignant and downright frightening, these stories could be read over an extended period with the young people in our schools. They have indelible impact and power.

Some may be familiar, some were written specifically for this collection. Each stands alone. The statistics that Mazer includes following the text remain in your mind long after the reading is done. Let us not be complacent enough to dare imagine that it only happens elsewhere.

Myers, Walter Dean *Monster*

The cover shows three medals — well deserved. This is not a "feel good" book. In fact, it is likely to leave us with questions that will remain unanswered. The style is just another example of the creative and thought-provoking genius of this writer. *Monster* is told through Steve's journal and the screenplay he intends to film to tell his story.

I found the disturbing images of young offenders in jail graphic and scary, and the drama of the courtroom very believable. The testimony is clear. We learn much about the defendant, his family and his neighborhood. Although there is a verdict when the trial is done, there is no resolution for the reader. The author leaves us with a decision to make on our own, based on all that he has given us in this inventive, yet disturbing novel.

Napoli, Donna Jo *The Magic Circle*

This commanding book was my introduction to Donna Napoli and her love of fairy tales.

In an unusual twist on the Hansel and Gretel story, we meet "The Ugly One," a hunchback midwife who receives the gift of healing when she learns to draw the magic circle. She is safe from demons within that circle. Through a trick she loses her powers to those very demons. Accused of witchcraft, she seeks refuge in the deepest forest and is able to forget her prior life, keeping her demons at bay. Enter Hansel and Gretel.

Told in perfectly chosen words, this short novel should lead you to each of Napoli's other innovative twists on familiar childhood tales.

> The best way to get the conversation going when you have shared any one of Donna Jo Napoli's fairy-tale novels is to seek the questions that Napoli asked herself before she was able to write from an entirely different perspective. Why did the witch live in a candy house in the forest? Why was she so far away from anyone else? Why would a woman want to eat children when she seemed to have all the food she needed?
>
> *The Magic Circle* is a great beginning. It is short and will certainly inspire further talk. But don't forget to read and booktalk her other exceptional novels. How tough was it for a prince to learn to live in the body of a beast? Why did Rumplestiltskin want to help the miller's daughter? What happened to Jack's father? Why would a mother want to isolate her daughter in a tower, and how would that isolation affect the girl?

Park, Linda Sue *A Single Shard*

Min is the greatest potter in the village and Tree-Ear is an orphan who admires Min's artistry and longs to learn his craft. When Min seeks a commission from the government to create state pottery, it is left to Tree-Ear to carry the assembled collection to the palace. He is set upon by robbers who throw his precious parcel down the mountainside. Seemingly faced with failure, Tree-Ear meets the challenge and gets the commission. Upon his return, he must come to grips with the death of his mentor and friend, Crane-Man. But his bravery and ingenuity are rewarded when Min agrees to be his teacher and invites him to make his home with the family. Set in twelfth century Korea and celebrating the Celadon pottery that was created there, this story is well researched and deserving of the accolades it has received since its publication.

Paterson, Katherine *Jip: His Story*

Katherine Paterson has created another character who makes us laugh and cry. Jip binds himself to us in true friendship. He has lived most of his life on a "poor farm," where he was placed when he fell off a passing wagon and no one returned for him. When a stranger tells him that he knows his father, Jip is apprehensive, yet he has always wanted to believe that his father was searching for him.

Disillusioned to learn that the anticipated reunion is with a slave hunter who wants to claim his son as property, Jip seeks counsel from his teacher, Lyddie (a familiar character from a previous novel). She helps him escape to Canada.

Protagonists whose chaotic childhoods seem destined to sweep them into the adult world too soon are Katherine Paterson's forte. She says they speak for her.

Randle, Kristen *Breaking Rank*

An absorbing and unusual story, this book is insightful in the wake of media reports from high schools where students are scorned and feared because they appear to be different.

Baby belongs to the Clan, a silent, enigmatic group that wears dark clothes and talks to no one. In the Clan he finds safety. When it is discovered that Baby is smart and should be put in an accelerated learning environment, Casey becomes his tutor. She is to help guide him into the mainstream. That move will prove threatening to the Clan and to the Cribs, the popular letter kids. Baby is told that if he steps outside, he will have to stay out. There is no going both ways. Baby and Casey must face the threats from both groups and try to find a new place in the world — together.

Rennison, Louise *Angus, Thongs and Full-Frontal Snogging*

Angus is Georgia's part-Scottish wildcat whose presence is felt in many of the journal entries that make up the book. Thongs are stupid underwear, and full-frontal snogging is kissing with all the trimmings. The book is hilariously funny and filled with all the angst that a fourteen-year-old girl can muster. Georgia is unsure of herself, her body, her ability to get a boyfriend and her relationships with her so-called friends. Nothing is easy. Her family is in turmoil, her friendships are wavering and her love for Robbie crowds out all normal thought. There is much to be savored here, much to read over and over. You may not want to read it in public, as it will cause you to laugh out loud at any number of junctures.

Toten, Teresa *The Game* ❧

Dani is in treatment for alcohol abuse and attempted suicide. As she participates in rehab she describes the game that is part of the life she lives with her sister, Kelly. The writing is bold and realistic, tugging at the reader's heart and holding us in its grip as we witness the events that are part of Dani's days at the clinic. We meet her as she faces her isolation at the center and follow as she sifts through the hazy memories that flood her consciousness. Finally, we come to realize all that she has experienced and what led her to this place in time. Powerful storytelling from a talented and accomplished writer! You will not soon forget those who people the pages of this fine novel.

Voigt, Cynthia *Homecoming*

I was introduced to Cynthia Voigt through this story about the Tillerman family of four children, abandoned by their mother in a shopping mall parking lot, and their quest to find a home. Dicey, the oldest, first takes them to a favored aunt who thinks that the only way to save them is to put them in foster care, a move that is sure to tear them apart. Dicey will not let that happen. So they sneak away and find themselves on another journey, this time to find their grandmother, who may be their only hope for staying together. The meeting is not celebratory, and the children and Grandma must come to terms with the fact that Grandma is reclusive and set in her ways. She is not about to change her life to meet their needs. They all must make changes if they are to create a new family.

Woodson, Jacqueline *if you come softly*

I sobbed as I finished this book about Ellie (Elisha, white Jewish girl) and Miah Jeremiah (black Christian boy). They are characters to love and cherish. They meet at a private school and fall in love. But racial mixing is taboo and they are constantly confronted with others' reaction to their love and friendship. This is a lovely and touching story of families who must deal with what is best for their children and with the realization that a love like this doesn't come along in every lifetime. Through alternating voices we come to know these characters intimately and to want what is best for them. Despite the secrets and setbacks, there is hope that they will enjoy a good life. Then time and circumstance change all that.

Wynne-Jones, Tim *Stephen Fair* ✻

Following up on the success of *The Maestro*, Tim Wynne-Jones creates another fifteen-year-old male struggling with terrifying events in his life. He seems to have inherited his brother Marcus's nightmares. They revolve around babies, fire and a treehouse. He cannot come to grips with their meaning. His friends try to help him deal with the mysteries that plague him. Then he visits his grandmother and discovers that Marcus has been staying with her, and he begins to unravel the threads that are his life. At last he can return home to his mother. Well-told and fast-paced, this is a story that stays with the reader for a long time.

Part IV: *Lucie Poulin-Mackey*

By the time they reach fifteen, young adults have developed a taste for particular authors and styles of writing. Being French Canadian, I've included books that depict French-Canadian lifestyles at the turn of the twentieth century. I've included a variety of genres (poetry, plays) for a wider range of choice. I've also included books that are considered classics in French-Canadian literature, such as those by Antonine Maillet and Gabrielle Roy. I hope that these books will create lasting memories for you as they did for me.

Cousture, Arlette *Les filles de Caleb : Tome 1, Le chant du coq* ✻

The author of the most famous love story ever told in French Canada is a direct descendant of the main character, Emilie Bordeleau. The oldest daughter of Caleb Bordeleau, Emilie becomes a teacher and falls in love with one of her students, Ovila. They eventually marry and lead a life of misery and hardship, kept together by their love for each other. After many years, Emilie leaves her beloved Ovila and tries to build a new life for herself and her children. Their love will never die, but they just can't live together. In 1990 this book and its sequel, *Blanche*, were made into a twenty-week TV series that captivated French-Canadian audiences and was translated for English Canada. No other series has had so much success. A must read for French-Canadian history buffs.

> I love antiques and am an avid collector. I think that I've been transported into the modern era from the time a century or so ago where I belong. Oil lamps and wood stoves are my thing. When *Les filles de Caleb* came out, I read it in two days. I have a confession to make: Hello, my name is Lucie, and I'm addicted to turn-of-the-century literature. I hope you are too.

Dalpé, Jean-Marc and Brigitte Haetjens
1932, La ville du nickel ❦

This play is set in my hometown, Sudbury, mining capital of the world. I couldn't pass it up. Jean-Marc Dalpé captivated his audience with this love story and the harsh reality of mining in this era. I grew up with a miner, so when I read this play I'm reminded of the smell of the underground, the smell of the sulfur in the air while playing outside before the big stack was built and the sight of the alluring lights of the slag dump. A poet and playwright, now novelist, Dalpé uses hard words and powerful images to take you to a mining town.

Demers, Dominique *Ta voix dans la nuit* ❦

At sixteen, Fanny is trying to adapt to a new school. She becomes the victim of cruel assaults by the "in" girls. Day after day she must deal with being dubbed "enemy number one." She holds her head high, but the anger builds inside her. Will someone help her and ultimately save her from her fragile self?

Desrochers, Pierre *Ma vie zigzague* ❦

Charles has one dream: to meet his idol, Patrick Roy. One day he gets his chance, only to have it stolen away. Stuck in bed with a bad fever, he learns that Roy has been traded to Colorado. The backdrop to this story is the St. Justine Hospital specializing in childhood diseases. Charles has bigger concerns than meeting his idol. A tale of coming to grips with life and death.

Durand, Frédérick *Le Carrousel pourpre* ❧

I think this is the only fantasy in all my lists. I'm not partial to this genre, but I thought it best to include one for those who are. One night Marie finds herself in a cemetery without her memory. Find out how a doll and a book help her to adjust to her new surroundings. A tale of ghosts and friendship.

Levine, Karen *La valise d'Hana*

Almost seventy years after the end of World War II, a director for the Holocaust Center in Japan received a suitcase with a label reading *Hana Brady. May 16th 1931. Orphan*. The suitcase is also marked *Auschwitz*. Fukimo Ishioka is determined to learn the young girl's story. A moving tale of determination and of history, this book has been translated into twenty languages and has received the Gold World Medal at the New York International Radio Festival and many other awards.

Lienhardt, Jean-Michel *Anne et Godefroy* ❧

First the Capulets and the Montagues, now Anne and Godefroy. A story of secret love set in the twelfth century in the time of horsemen and castles, when honor and chivalry reigned supreme. Two young adults fall in love despite their families being sworn enemies. Follow their love affair to the bitter end. Will it flourish or will they abandon their love for the greater good of the families?

Maillet, Antonine *La Sagouine* ❧

One of French Canada's most celebrated authors, Mme Maillet hails from the small New Brunswick village of Bouctouche. This is her first published work, a one-woman play about an Acadian cleaning lady who cannot read and write, but whose views on the world are poignant and make us think.

Ouimet, Josée *L'orpheline de la maison Chevalier* ✤

After her mother's death, Marie is sent to work for Monsieur Chevalier in order to pay off her family's debts. The story is set in 1753 in the city of Québec. Marie finds the work very hard and survives only on her uncle's promise that she will be home for Christmas.

Paul *Placide, l'homme mystérieux, à New York* ✤
Retold by Gilbert Buote

From January 21 to August 18, 1904, a police adventure called *Placide, l'homme mystérieux* was serialized in *L'Impartial*, the local newspaper in Tignish, P.E.I. The committee for the bicentennial celebrations of Tignish have published the series as a book to present it to young readers and to celebrate the fact that it is more than likely the first Acadian novel ever published.

Porée-Kurrer, Philippe *La promise du lac* ✤

One hundred years ago, a Frenchman wrote one of Canada's classics, *Maria Chapdelaine*. In that story set in the Lac St-Jean area, Louis Hémon wrote of a girl's love and hardship in the harsh Canadian land at the turn of the century. Many years later another Frenchman from Normandy wrote a sequel to this tale of adventure, family life and self-discovery. He also fell in love with the country, its customs, its nature and, most of all, its people. Married to a native of Lac St-Jean, Porée-Kurrer continues Maria's story and adds unexpected twists to a century-old tale. A must read. A new classic is born.

Prévert, Jacques *Paroles*

This French poet is like no other. He made fun of government, institutions and authority in general. I fell in love with his rebellious style at university, and to this day I read one of his poems to graduating classes. His commitment to justice for children and for everyone is very appealing. My all-time favorite of his poems is "Pour faire le portrait d'un oiseau." A different style of poetry encompassing humor and sarcasm.

Rouy, Maryse *Jordan et la Forteresse assiégée* ✤

Set in medieval times, this story follows the adventures of Jordan, who must leave his family to train as a knight. On the way, he meets up with a band of villains who mean harm to him and to the castle he must protect. The author is a specialist in medieval history. Find Jordan in other adventures by the same author.

Roy, Gabrielle *Bonheur d'occasion* ❧

Set in the village of St. Henri, where everyone is looking for happiness. Some try to find it with their family, others try to find it in the war, others will search forever. Originally from St. Boniface, Manitoba, Roy lived briefly in Montreal and was able to capture the essence of the times, the people, the places and the culture. Translated into many languages and captured on film, this is the best of her works. To this day, years after her death, Gabrielle Roy is the grande dame of Canadian literature.

Stanké, Claudie and Daniel M. Vincent
15, rue des Embuscades ❧

In this first-person account, the author finds himself at the bottom of a stairwell with a gun in his hand. Did he commit the crime? From his hiding place, he communicates with his sister who is at the head of the investigation to clear his name. Will she succeed or is it too late? A police drama that will captivate all.

CHAPTER SEVEN

Seasonal Books

Part 1: *David Bouchard*

THANKSGIVING

Jackson, Alison *I Know an Old Lady Who Swallowed a Pie* (Preschool)

You can't go wrong combining a familiar rhyme with almost anything. Here, Jackson plugs her humor into traditional Thanksgiving foods. Sweet!

HALLOWE'EN

San Souci, Robert *Cinderella Skeleton* (Primary)

This beautiful book has a taste of Tim Burton's book, *The Nightmare Before Christmas*. The title tells all, including making us wonder if Cinderella's skeleton wouldn't leave her entire foot behind as she escapes the prince's ball. This is a Hallowe'en rhythm-and-rhyme sweetie that is exceptionally well illustrated by David Catrow. There aren't enough Hallowe'en picture books for my liking. This one works for me and for my daughter.

CHRISTMAS

Briggs, Raymond *The Snowman* (Preschool)

The story of a snowman who invites a young boy to fly with him to his world (and to meet Santa) is a classic wordless picture book that all young children should have in their libraries. I can't imagine anyone not wanting to own the movie as well. They are equally pleasing. Victoria enjoys them as much in the summer as she does at Christmas.

Bunting, Eve *Night Tree* (Preschool/Primary)

This is a moving story about a family that goes into the forest every

Christmas to decorate the same tree with edible strings and balls. They put the decorations together for a special group come Christmas. Which group, you ask?

Burton, Tim *The Nightmare Before Christmas*
(Primary/Intermediate)
My wife, Vicki, was somewhat upset when she found me reading Burton's picture book to our three-year-old daughter. Was the notion of Jack Skellington's taking Santa Claws captive and trying to spread fear at Christmas not appropriate for a two-year-old? My Vicki was even more upset when she found us watching the video of the book. Victoria loved both. I love both. The book is as wonderful as the movie!

Cooney, Caroline *What Child Is This?* (Intermediate/Young Teen)
Do not attempt to read this book without a full box of tissues by your side. Vicki and I needed three different readings to get through the last six pages of this moving YA Christmas novel of a young girl hoping against all hopes for her Christmas wish to come true.

Liz could not stop reading the bells.
Ryan, age 6, wants action toys, a baseball mitt,
and Matchbox cars.
Lori, age 4, wants a baby doll with hair she can comb.
Katie, age 8, wants a family.
Liz stepped back from that one.
Katie, age 8, wants a family.

Hegg, Tom *A Cup of Christmas Tea* (Intermediate to Adult)
One million readers have made the story of a man's Christmas coming to life through little more than tea at an old aunt's a part of their families' most cherished tradition. Can a million readers be wrong?

Major, Kevin *The House of Wooden Santas* ✤
(Primary/Intermediate)
My friend and colleague from Newfoundland won the Mr. Christie

Award for his story of a single mom trying to make a living by carving Christmas Santas. Her challenges are compounded by everything her young son feels at this time of the year. The illustrations are photographs of wonderful woodcarvings by Acadian carver Imelda George. One of George's wooden Santas stands on our mantle, right next to the book. You can contact her for one of your own, one more way of adding to the magic of books.

Polacco, Patricia *Christmas Tapestry* (Primary)
A poignant holiday tale of two families, two faiths and two lonely people united by a beautiful twist of fate. Another that brought a tear to my eye, which is easier than not, particularly with Christmas books.

Rylant, Cynthia *The Children of Christmas* (Primary/Intermediate)
I've yet to read this series of short Christmas stories to any group without success. I often say that Cynthia Rylant is my favorite author, and this little treasure is one of the reasons that I do. Tissues needed!

Slate, Joseph *Who Is Coming to Our House?* (Preschool)
When the animals prepare for Christmas, who do you think they are getting ready to receive? This touching short story is ideally presented as a board book. Its depiction of the birth of baby Jesus is perfectly sweet.

Van Allsburg, Chris *The Polar Express* (All ages)
If I had only one Christmas book, this classic telling of a child's trip aboard the Polar Express would be the one. As you'd expect, the train runs to and from Santa's home. That children ride the train is hardly surprising. That one returns home with something from Santa's sleigh is not expected. A must own for all.

Wojciechowski, Susan *The Christmas Miracle of Jonathan Toomey* (All ages)
Like *The Polar Express*, this is a touching classic that you will want to read again and again and again. If your children enjoy it, all the better. Watching you sob your way through a picture book about a sad woodcarver

who can hardly endure life without his wife and child will speak volumes about the importance and enjoyment of reading.

Part II: *Anne Letain*

VALENTINE'S DAY

Gillmor, Don *Yuck, A Love Story* (Primary) ❦

More award-winning magic from the author/illustrator team of Don Gillmor and Marie-Louise Gay. Austin Grouper has a problem — reconciling the idea that girls are yucky with the fact that the girl of his dreams has moved in next door. When all of Austin's efforts to gain Amy's attention fail miserably, Austin decides he must bring Amy the moon, no matter what. Gay's zany and colorful watercolors are a perfect match for Gillmor's dry wit.

EASTER

Hoban, Russell *Egg Thoughts, and Other Frances Songs* (Primary)

Egg Thoughts cannot really be designated an Easter title, but is rather a compilation of some of the best Frances-the-badger songs from the Frances books by Russell Hoban (*A Bargain for Frances, Bread and Jam for Frances*, etc.) The Frances books are classics in their own right, and Frances's personal philosophy on life as reflected in her poetry is always a delight. "Egg Thoughts" is the perfect Easter poem. The rest of the collection can be enjoyed throughout the year by young and old alike.

SOFT-BOILED

I do not like the way you slide,
I do not like your soft inside,
I do not like you many ways,
And I could do for many days
Without a soft-boiled egg.

Wells, Rosemary *Max's Chocolate Chicken* (Primary)

Max and Ruby are back in fine form as the defiant little brother and the bossy big sister. This time it's Easter, and Max and Ruby are on an Easter egg hunt. Naturally Max finds everything but Easter eggs, and Ruby is gloating. Never fear! Max delivers an appropriate comeuppance. The book exudes charm and fun and begs to be enjoyed every year. Max, Ruby, Easter, chocolate — who can ask for more?

MOTHER'S DAY

Loewen, Iris *My Mom Is So Unusual* (Primary) 🍁

This is that rare book that addresses the relationship between a single mother and her only daughter. It is a celebration of the bond between mother and child in a refreshing book that realistically depicts life as a large segment of Canadian children experience it. May be hard to find, but definitely worth the hunt.

Mayer, Mercer *Just for You* (Primary)

Absolutely the best of the Little Critter books, *Just for You* is the perfect Mother's Day vehicle for a toddler or young child. Gentle and child empathetic in concept, it has become a classic kid's book — and a classic that is often available at the local grocery store. The end will bring a tear to any mother's eye.

This book may just be "the" title that ignited my interest in and passion for kids' books. I was teaching special education in Edmonton when I happened to attend an in-service presented by another resource room teacher. Her whole presentation turned on a light bulb for me regarding inspiring kids to learn rather than drilling them to death with rote activities. This phenomenal teacher had used *Just for You* as the impetus to get her challenged students to write. For the first time in my teaching career, I considered using a real book to teach with rather than a teachers' guide or manual. Needless to say, I flew to a local bookstore to buy the book, and I suppose that you could say that I've never looked back.

HALLOWE'EN

Fox, Mem *Guess What?* (Primary)

Guess What? is a picture book that almost defies description — it's a witches' brew of pop culture, Hallowe'en, favorite book characters and a worthy message! It is brilliant in its very simplicity and always leads to reader participation. Vivienne Goodman's pictures leap off the pages and beg for closer examination.

Sierra, Judy *The House That Drac Built* (Primary)

Noted storyteller Judy Sierra has created a Hallowe'en version of the familiar cumulative rhyme "The House That Jack Built." Sierra employs astoundingly memorable language to build to her climax, which culminates in a surprise ending. Will Hillenbrand's lively but not overly dark illustrations are a perfect complement to Sierra's poetry.

Wood, Audrey *Heckedy Peg* (Primary)

Heckedy Peg is the best witch story ever. It is deep and dark and embraces everything that is Hallowe'en, including a spell that only a mother can break. Don Wood's stunning paintings are luminous with unusual light and eerie detail and need to be examined scrupulously. An ultimate marriage of word and illustration, *Heckedy Peg* is exemplary in every way.

Ziefert, Harriet *Scare the Moon* (Primary)

Scare the Moon takes a simple and repetitive concept and emerges as an attractive and fun pop-up book that kids just love. Basically, Griselda the Witch and George the Warlock are having a contest to see who can "boo" the loudest. There are great opportunities for anticipation and chiming in. Great for group reading and just a whole bunch of laughter.

I can hardly wait to get to Hallowe'en to share this book with my first graders. I divide them into a girls' group and a boys' group and then get them booing to their full lung capacity as I pit them against each other. I know I've done a really good job when the teachers on either side of my school library send out someone to close both their doors and mine! And to think I found the book at Liquidation World!

Remembrance Day

Granfield, Linda *In Flanders Fields — The Story of the Poem by John McRae* (Upper Elementary and up) ❧

Linda Granfield filled a big void when she produced this wonderful book about the poem "In Flanders Fields" — a poem that just about every Canadian child gains more than a passing acquaintance with in school. Granfield's research is impeccable and she is always respectful of her young audience. Janet Wilson's paintings are an awesome tribute to the poem. Equally useful is Granfield's *Where Poppies Grow*, which gives young people an accurate depiction of World War I through photos, anecdotes and memorabilia.

Christmas

Breathed, Berkeley *A Wish for Wings That Work* (Primary)

Opus the Penguin has but one wish in life — to fly! Like most of us, Opus believes that if you ask Santa for a special present with true hope in your heart, your dreams may come true. The story of Opus's Christmas, told and illustrated by well-known American illustrator and cartoonist Berkeley Breathed, will entertain, amuse and demonstrate the true spirit of Christmas.

Fox, Mem *Wombat Divine* (Primary)

A Christmas treat from Australia, *Wombat Divine* is sure to become an enduring favorite. Wombat has waited forever to be part of the annual nativity play, but at the auditions it becomes apparent that there may not be an appropriate part for him in the play. Readers will be rooting for Wombat from the first page, and this celebration of Australian animals at Christmas is enlightening and enjoyable for those of us who live on the other side of the big pond.

Gillmor, Don *The Christmas Orange* (Primary/Intermediate) ❧

Anton Stingley was born on Christmas Day and thinks he should be getting double the loot. When all he receives for Christmas is a single orange, he decides to sue Santa. Through a series of eye-opening and humorous events, Anton discovers the error of his ways and the true meaning of Christmas. Only Gillmor could name a lawyer Wiley Studpustle, and once again Marie-Louise Gay's illustrations are pure pleasure. Now also available as a movie on video or DVD.

Herriot, James *The Christmas Day Kitten* (Primary)

This beautiful and tender story by master storyteller James Herriot is a quiet keeper. It is the story of a stray and sickly cat that arrives at a Yorkshire farmhouse on Christmas Day carrying a newborn kitten. Both sad and triumphant, the book is wonderfully illustrated by Ruth Brown and should find a place in hearts of all ages.

Wells, Rosemary *Morris's Disappearing Bag* (Primary)

Rosemary Wells' humorous take on family life rarely fails to endear and entertain. Combining Christmas, magic and getting your family to disappear is irresistible. As usual, Wells shows imagination, zest and wit in the illustrations. Morris is especially appealing in this warmly satisfying story that kids beg to hear over and over again.

Part III: *Sally Bender*

When I was asked to name some of my favorite seasonal books, I knew that I was in trouble. My basement shelves are filled with books that I read or have read to our kids or to the kids at school at special times of the year. They are some of my all-time favorite read alouds. The difficulty has been in cutting the list to fit this book. I have chosen books for a variety of special days, including birthdays. Apart from Christmas and Hallowe'en, there is no more important time in the lives of our young ones than their own personal celebration.

BIRTHDAYS

Look, Lenore *Henry's First-Moon Birthday* (Primary)

Jen's baby brother does nothing but eat, sleep and cry. Still, it is his one-month birthday and the family is gathering to celebrate. GrinGrin and

Jen are in charge. They prepare the traditional foods and write good-luck messages in ink. The relatives arrive to share in Henry's special day. Jen knows that one day Henry will be happy that she was in charge when the time for his first-month birthday rolled around. This is a warm family celebration in the Chinese tradition, and it is aptly portrayed in detail-filled pencil-oil-collage illustrations.

Scrimger, Richard *Bun Bun's Birthday* (Primary) ❀

Imagine Winifred's surprise when she discovers that the fancy cake and all the hoopla being planned are for her wee sister, Bun Bun, on her first birthday. Winifred is not happy to be relegated to second fiddle. She exiles herself to the closet and it takes some fast talking on her mother's part to convince her that Winifred, too, had a first birthday. Bun Bun will need someone to let her know what happened at the special celebration as she gets older. Who will take on that job?

CHINESE NEW YEAR

Wallace, Ian *Chin Chiang and the Dragon's Dance* (Primary/Intermediate) ❀

Chin Chiang has always dreamed of dancing the dragon's dance with his grandfather, but now the time has come and he is scared. He knows that he will bring honor to his family if his dance is pleasing. The dragon will bring prosperity to his family for the coming year. But what if he stumbles? Chin Chiang runs away rather than take that chance. On the rooftop he meets a new friend, Pu Yee, who helps him practice his part. With some trepidation, Chin Chiang takes his place at the tail. He proves that he can dance the part and continues the celebration with his family and new friend. What a celebration!

VALENTINE'S DAY

Carrick, Carol *Valentine* (Primary)

Heather is upset when her mother must go to work and cannot spend Valentine's Day with her. Grandma tries to distract her with the baking of Valentine cookies, but the real distraction comes when the two head to the barn to check on Clover and her newborn lambs. They are dismayed to find one cold and motionless. They must care for the baby when the mother is unable to do so, a parallel story to the one played out by Heather and her grandmother. Infusing this family story with factual information, Carrick provides a welcome addition to your collection of holiday books.

EASTER

Polacco, Patricia *Chicken Sunday* (Intermediate)

Miss Eula Mae has a voice like "slow thunder and sweet rain." She uses it every Sunday at the Baptist church where she takes her grandsons and often their neighbor, Trisha. On the way home from church she savors the hat-making of Mr. Kodinski and spies a hat that she would love to own. The children decide to buy it for her, but must come up with an idea to earn the money. A misunderstanding leads them to work out a deal with the proprietor, and in doing so, they remind him of his Ukrainian homeland. Miss Eula gets her Easter bonnet and we get a wonderful story that celebrates the African-American and Russian-Jewish traditions of its characters.

MOTHER'S DAY

Balian, Lorna *Mother's Mother's Day* (Primary)

In a mouse family there are many living generations. When Hazel sets out to take her mother a small gift for Mother's Day, she is surprised to find her tree-trunk home empty. It seems that Mother has set off to see her mother. She, too, does not find her mother at home. She has gone to see *her* mother. And so on, and so on . . .

A lovely little tale that reminds us that mothers have mothers (and they all have names). Though they live apart, they love each other. Let the celebration begin!

FATHER'S DAY

Bridges, Margaret Park *If I Were Your Father* (Primary)

A close father-son relationship shows what might happen if the traditional roles of parent and child were reversed. The boy would shave with whipped cream and brush his teeth with cake frosting. All the glorious, imaginative things that kids would do, if only they had parent power. They go about the chores of the day as they discuss and imagine how their lives might change. At the end of the day they are back to their real place in the family structure, and we know that they have something very special. Pair it with *If I Were Your Mother* for a full family adventure.

THANKSGIVING

Cowley, Joy *Gracias, the Thanksgiving Turkey*
(Primary/Intermediate)

Miguel's father is a truck driver and Miguel is worried that he won't be home in time to celebrate Thanksgiving with his family. Papa sends him a turkey and tells him "to fatten it up" for their dinner. Of course, Miguel falls in love with Gracias and treats him as a pet, a pet that follows Miguel everywhere, even to church, where he is blessed by the parish priest. Miguel is sure that they will not be able to serve a blessed turkey for dinner. He is, of course, right, and Gracias is a guest at the table, not on it.

HALLOWE'EN

Martin, Bill, Jr. *The Ghost-Eye Tree* (All ages)

I have read this book countless times and I never tire of it. The beauty of the spooky night and the delicious use of warm yellow light and gray-black shadow add just the right touch of tension to a story whose rich language tells of a brother and sister sent out on a windswept night to collect some milk from "the edge of the town." To get to Mr. Cowlander's, they must pass the ghost-eye tree, and they are scared. Brother wears a slouch hat pulled down over his eyes to make him look tough. Sister says it makes him look stupid. What will they do after he loses it as they scramble home in terror when the tree moans as they pass by?

Merriam, Eve *Spooky ABC* (Intermediate/Teen)

This book is the epitome of spooky! When Lane Smith drew his illustrations, he intended to publish them as a wordless book. But they begged for macabre words to enhance the drama of the paintings. Enter noted poet Eve Merriam. What a collaborative team, as evidenced by the first poem. An auspicious start to a book designed for the brave-hearted. This duo leaves no rock unturned in their attempt to scare the wits out of their readers.

> *Apple: Delicious/malicious/one bite and/you're dead.*

DIVALI

Gilmore, Rachna *Lights for Gita* (Primary/Intermediate) ❦

Divali is the festival of lights for the Hindus of the world. It is a celebration that honors Lakshimi, Goddess of Wealth. If she is pleased, the year to follow will be filled with good fortune and prosperity.

Gita is missing New Delhi and the family that she and her parents left behind when they came to Canada. She is wishing she had never come. There will be no fireworks because of the freezing rain that is falling. Her friends cannot get to her party because of icy streets. Nothing will ever be the same! Her mother reminds her that Divali is not about fireworks, but about filling the darkness with light. That they do and she is able to appreciate the beauty of the festival. Now Gita cannot wait to tell her grandparents about her first celebration of Divali in her new home.

REMEMBRANCE DAY

Trottier, Maxine *Flags* (Primary/Intermediate) ❦

On a visit to the West Coast, Mary stays with her grandmother and meets Mr. Hiroshi, who lives next door. Mr. Hiroshi has a beautiful garden and Mary is attracted to the peace and serenity that he has created within the garden's space. Then one day the soldiers come and take Mr. Hiroshi away to an internment camp. Mary promises to take care of his garden for him. The house is sold, and Mary removes two iris bulbs and one stone in hopes of creating a garden in remembrance of her friend. A wise introduction to the events that followed the war and a great companion book to *Baseball Saved Us*.

Tsuchiya, Yukio *Faithful Elephants* (All ages)

No book has the impact that this one has when you speak with children about the effects of war. They have empathy for, and an affinity with, animals that allow a heartfelt response to the plight of the elephants that inhabited the Tokyo Zoo while the bombs were being dropped during World War II. The fear that the elephants would get loose and rampage through city streets led to the destruction of these brave and intelligent creatures. Children are distraught to think of their fate. It is a story that needs to be shared, but with a tissue close at hand.

> When my school decided to make the focus of our Remembrance Day service more relevant to the young children who attend our school, I chose to read *Faithful Elephants*. Knowing the empathy that children have for animals, I felt that the elephants' sad story would have an impact on their thinking about war . . . helping them to realize that war always affects the innocent and the defenceless. I practiced and practiced until I could read it without tears (and the occasional sob), only to start crying while I was standing in front of the audience and sharing the pleas of the keepers as they helplessly watched their poisoned friends die. One of my kindergarten kids tugged my pant leg, touched my hand when I leaned down to see what the problem was, and politely asked, "Mrs. Bender, do you know you're crying?"

HANUKKAH

Kimmel, Eric *Hershel and the Hanukkah Goblins* (All ages)

I usually bring someone running when I read this story to the kids in my school. They are alarmed by all the noise and yelling. It is a tale filled with the great characters of the goblins and especially of Hershel. When the goblins try, once again, to spoil Hanukkah for the residents of Ostropol, it is up to Hershel to save their celebration. He doesn't need weapons to defeat the holiday-hating goblins; he needs brainpower. The story of his battle with a succession of smarmy, joyless apparitions is told with great skill and makes this a book that is requested throughout the school year.

CHRISTMAS

Allan, Nicholas *Jesus' Christmas Party* (All ages)

Told from the point of view of the innkeeper, who liked nothing better than a good night's sleep, this is a rollicking retelling of the Christmas story. The nighttime visitors get no special treatment from him when they need a place to stay. Along come shepherds and wise men. Finally, what are those angels doing? It is, without a doubt, my favorite read aloud of the season and is always requested by children and adults alike.

> I was once invited to our senior administration office to read to the staff at their annual Christmas luncheon. I thought long and hard about what book I would take with me. At that time I had a special favorite called *Karin's Christmas Walk* (out of print) that I loved to read. I felt that I would cry (all over again) when I shared it, so I decided to take *Jesus' Christmas Party*. I knew it would be a hit and provide the entertainment needed as we celebrated the Christmas season together. That must have been ten years ago, and people still stop me to remind me how much they enjoyed the reading and how they have since bought that very book for their children or grandchildren or friends.

Burningham, John *Harvey Slumfenburger's Christmas Present* (Preschool/Primary)

What a great read for young children! When Santa arrives back at the North Pole, he discovers that he has forgotten to deliver one present, likely the only present that Harvey Slumfenburger will receive. One of the reindeer is sick and they are all tired, so Santa sets off on his own to make the last delivery. He gets a lot of help along the way, and the gift reaches its destination just as the sun is peeking over the eastern horizon. Whew!

Krensky, Stephen *How Santa Got His Job* (Intermediate)

This picture book is really appropriate for older, more sophisticated readers. Their ability to catch the humor and note the clues that the author provides makes it most enjoyable for them. All those jobs that Santa has prior to accepting the job of gift delivery prove useful to him. From being a chimney sweep to delivering mail in the middle of the night, he comes well equipped for the grueling Christmas Eve trek that he must take yearly.

Oppel, Kenneth *Follow That Star* (Primary/Intermediate) 🍁
Another favorite read aloud. In this book Oppel has done what all good authors can do for their readers. He provides us with a mystery and the clues that we need to predict what is going to happen in this wonderful story about the shepherds and the star they sight on Christmas Eve. He adds humor and memorable characters. In the end, we are left to savor the joy they all felt when they arrived in Bethlehem.

"Zach wasn't even there when the angels came."

Pearson, Tracey Campbell *Where Does Joe Go?* (Preschool/Primary)
The townspeople are delighted when Joe opens his snack shack for the spring and summer. They love his hot dogs, French fries and ice cream. But, come fall, Joe boards up the snack bar and disappears. It is left to his customers to guess what he might be doing. Perhaps he is in the swamp, tossing his wares to crusty crocs, or might he be digging for bones? It is anyone's guess, and guess they do.

But he always returns, red-cheeked, rotund and ready to serve. On the last page, we get a welcome surprise! Kids love such endings and you will too.

Part IV: *Lucie Poulin-Mackey*

MYTHS AND LEGENDS

Many myths and legends are well known among French Canadians. That's why I thought to include some in this list.

Anfousse, Ginette *L'Hiver ou le Bonhomme Sept-Heures* 🍁
(Preschool/Primary)
Have you ever heard of le bonhomme Sept-Heures? In English this beast is known as the tame sandman. Not in French Canada. His reputation was enough to send kids to bed early to avoid him. In this cute story,

Ginette Anfousse perpetuates this legend through the eyes of Jiji, a young girl with a big imagination. Not to worry; he's not real.

Cayla, Fabrice *Le guide illustré des mythes et des légendes* (Intermediate)

In this non-fiction book, a multitude of fantastic beasts, creatures, princesses and giants are described, demystified and accounted for. They are regrouped according to more than thirty categories and span five continents. If you need to enrich your literary knowledge of such creatures, you have found your book.

VALENTINE'S DAY

McBratney, Sam *Devine combien je t'aime*
Translated by Claude Lager (Preschool/Primary)

I love you THIS much. Big brown bunny and little brown bunny have a match to find out who loves who more. Their love has no boundaries. An endearing story of love and friendship.

Waddell, Martin *Dis-moi qui tu aimes . . .*
French text by Marie-France Floury (Primary)

It is bedtime and Tina the cat plays the same game with her mom every night. Mom always asks, "Who do you love?" and Tina announces her list, keeping Mom till the end. A cute bedtime story.

MAPLE SUGAR TIME

Since maple sugar time is a precious tradition in French Canada, I thought it best to add some reading materials to the list.

Crook, Connie Brummel *Lune d'érable* ❦
French text by Marie-Andrée Clermont (Primary/Intermediate)

Many legends have been told of the discovery of maple syrup. This book is a retelling of the legends. As in tales of old, a First Nations woman cooks with sugar water, and an elder watches a squirrel, but most of the story is told in the author's own way. Celebrating the young boy's discovery, this legend is also a tale of the Mississauga tribe. Beautifully illustrated, the story sweeps the reader away with the force of the language and images. You feel the ancestors talking in the wind. Come and discover the beginning of an all-Canadian tradition, maple sugar.

Carney, Margaret *L'érablière de mon grand-père* 🍁
French text by Cécile Gagnon (Primary/Intermediate)

We are transported to a time when sugar water was collected by hand, manual labor at its finest. Discover the relationship between a grandfather and his grandson in this masterfully illustrated book. The images tell the story of traditional maple syrup-making, all the while showcasing nature in spring. A must for your collection.

HALLOWE'EN

Beaumont, Émilie *L'imagerie des sorcières et des fées* (Primary)
This is a collection of pictures and definitions surrounding the theme of Hallowe'en, such as witches' domains, their clothes, their friends, their formulas, their pastimes and much more. Brightly illustrated and easy to read, this will soon become your child's favorite.

Bourgeois, Paulette *Benjamin fête l'Halloween* 🍁
French text by Christiane Duchesne (Primary)

Here I go again with my favorite turtle. Yes, I must admit that I love Franklin in any adventure. So here he is in his first Hallowe'en story. Franklin, called Benjamin in the French version, goes about finding a costume and preparing for the big night, with no idea that it is not going to be an ordinary Hallowe'en. Let's just say that a ghost is involved. A spooky tale of friendship.

Ray, Mary Lyn *Le champ de M. Smith* (Primary)
M. Smith has always dreamt of owning a big piece of land and cultivating it. One day the opportunity presents itself. He decides to plant pumpkins. He soon realizes that reaping what you sow may come with a price. A tale of self-discovery and the benefits of hard work.

Surget, Alain *Le bal des sorcières* (Primary)
Okay, this one is just silly reading, but I'm including it anyway because

we need silly stories once in a while. This is a story of a witch who wants to become the queen of all witches. She orders from the witches' catalogue items that she thinks will make her just that. It doesn't work out as she planned. Will she ever become the queen? Find out.

CHRISTMAS

Deulceux, Marc (Editor) *Le Noël des artistes* ❦
(Intermediate to Adult)

This is a collection of stories told to Marc Deulceux by many French-Canadian artists including Ginette Reno, Gilles Vigneault and Roch Voisine. They share their fondest memories of funny events, Christmas traditions and anecdotes that are sure to please one and all.

Guérette, Charlotte (Editor) *La bûche de Noël* (All ages)
A collection of five traditional Christmas stories. You will find recollections of *la bûche de Noël*, *le loup garou* and the tradition of engagement at midnight mass. Come, listen to these stories by the fireside.

Pef *Motordu est le frère Noël* (All ages)
In this story we meet Prince Motordu's family and learn how his children deal with the issue of Santa Claus. Do they still believe in him? They would decorate the Christmas bunny with golden chickens and carrot lights. On Christmas Eve, wouldn't you know it, Santa knocks at their door the minute the children have gone to bed. Poor Santa's sleigh is broken and he needs help. If you love playing with words and are fond of Christmas, this will tickle your funny bone.

Timmermans, Félix *Un bateau du ciel*
Translated from German by Jean Fugère (All ages)

If this is not a classic, I don't know what is. A language masterpiece supported by high-caliber oil paintings, this is a beautiful story. Our children need to be challenged by words, and this tale does just that. Through this masterful book, you will discover certain European traditions surrounding St. Nicholas. This is the story of poor little Cécile and how her dream is realized along with those of others.

CHAPTER EIGHT

Resources for Administrators, Teachers and Parents

Part 1: *David Bouchard*

Barron, Marlene
I Learn to Read and Write the Way I Learn to Talk

Whole language is the official enemy in educational America. The problem with accepting the American way of treating children like any other commodity is that children are all different. This philosophy has crossed Canadian borders and caught on, much to the shame of a country that has traditionally known better. How can we hang our hats on the notion of standardized tests when we know that there is no such thing as a standard child? In this tiny treasure you can read what a successful American early-childhood educator has come to learn in her lifetime commitment to teaching young children to read.

Bialostok, Steven *Raising Readers:*
Helping Your Child to Literacy

Another book in which whole-language educators plead a case that makes too much sense to ignore.

Booth, David *Even Hockey Players Read*

My friend and colleague is widely accepted as one of Canada's foremost authorities on children's literature. In this book, David addresses the right way, not the easy way, to approach reading with all children, particularly boys who have their own ways of learning to read AND their own reading preferences.

Booth, David and Jennifer Rowsell *The Literacy Principle*

Educational administrators need the support of this book, the shot in the arm that it provides. If it is difficult for teachers to get excited about the teaching of reading, it is equally challenging for administrators who have to report to a system that is not interested in turning students into lifelong readers.

Goodman, Vera *Reading Is More Than Phonics!*

There are many tiny treasures to be found as we seek the right path to creating lifelong readers. Goodman's parents' guide for reading is one of these treasures. The title tells all; however, a quotation that Goodman drew from the Alberta Program of Studies for 1942 is too telling not to highlight: "Please teacher, don't teach the beginner to read by the phonics method. This method is long out-of-date. It is based on the idea that in reading, the reader moves his eyes from one letter to the next, sounding out the word. A good reader does not move his eyes in this way and no child should have this bad habit fixed upon him. It makes his reading slower in speed and poorer in comprehension."

Kohn, Alfie *Punished by Rewards*

Kohn focuses on something that our hearts have told us forever, but that has not until now been proven through meaningful and thoughtful research. This is a MUST for every professional and parent.

Kohn, Alfie *The Schools Our Children Deserve*

Parents, administrators and teachers: You MUST own this book. If you read but one, let it be this one. Read it again and again. Keep your highlighter at hand. In fact, get several in a variety of colors. You'll need them. Alfie has spent years researching and writing about what many of us have learned in our lifetimes as educators. Everything that Alfie writes, I've witnessed, as have many others. By American standards, Kohn is a maverick, a radical. By Canadian standards, Alfie Kohn is a visionary with courage, insight and nothing but the best interest of children at heart. Kohn is my hero! I wish he'd step away from his work in research and writing to start a school. I'd be the first to move into his catchment so that my daughter, Victoria, might be privy to his philosophy. America, why aren't you listening to him?

Krashen, Stephen *The Power of Reading*
One of the foremost world authorities on reading answers many questions in a clear and precise way.

Kropp, Paul *The Reading Solution:*
Make Your Child a Reader for Life
I owe my colleague and friend thanks for his work, particularly for his leading me to the three R's in getting students to become readers for life: Rule the television. Read with your children. Reach into your pockets.

Ungerleider, Charles *Failing Our Kids:*
How We Are Ruining Our Public Schools
This Canadian educator and former deputy minister of education searches deep in his own experiences and shares what many would prefer not to hear. He looks at the ongoing conflict between "traditional" and "progressive" approaches to education. He argues that the public school curriculum has become bloated, fragmented and mired in trivia. He takes on school choice and competition, where, more than anywhere else, rhetoric prevails over reason. Alfie Kohn? Not really, but clearly consistent with much of what Canadians tend to be—humane, caring and ready to say that which needs be said.

Part II: *Anne Letain*

Achuka (www.achuka.co.uk)
Self-described as a chock-full, eyes-peeled, independent children's book site, *Achuka* is a feast for children's book lovers of all ages. British in origin, it also addresses Canadian and American titles and has just about everything—from chatrooms to weblogs to extensive databases and links to other great sites. David Brown's *Children's Literature Web Guide* is also very good but has not been kept as up-to-date as *Achuka*, which is now in its seventh year and showing off a new and edgy format.

Bauer, Caroline Feller *Presenting Reader's Theatre*

Reader's theatre is a wonderful tool for getting kids into books, and nobody breaks down good children's literature and poetry like Caroline Feller Bauer. She also seems to know instinctively just what to pick to tickle kids' funny bones. There are other reader's theatre compilations around, but this is THE one to access. Caroline Feller Bauer has produced a plethora of books about exciting kids to read; another particular favorite is *This Way to Books*.

Canadian Materials (www.umanitoba.ca/cm)

CM is likely the oldest journal of reviews of Canadian materials for young people around. It existed first as a print journal, but now is only available in a free, on-line edition. Husbanded meticulously by the University of Manitoba's David Jenkinson, it is published every two weeks and provides pretty timely reviews by reputable reviewers of most that is new in Canada. It has a remarkable archive that I use frequently, and there is also an archive of the extensive interviews that Dave has done with Canadian authors of works for young people over the years. Reviews of books for children have dwindled dramatically over the past few years, so kudos to Dave and his volunteers for keeping *CM* alive and maintaining a high-quality product.

Carnegie and Greenaway Awards web site
(www.carnegiegreenaway.org.uk)

The beauty of this web site is the shadowing program that the organization has developed for the titles on the shortlist for the Carnegie Awards. Due to maturity and experience, we adults often have a different take on what is good to read and what is good for young people to read. On this site, thousands of kids registered in shadowing groups for the Carnegie shortlist of best young adult books get to post their opinions on the selected titles. Each title averages close to 2000 reviews/opinions, and it is both enlightening and refreshing to read what kids are really thinking about books. I just wish we could do something similar with our Govenor General's shortlist or CLA Book of the Year shortlist in Canada. The readers' choice lists done in most provinces are too disparate to get a consensal feel for what kids really, really like.

Children's Book News *(www.bookcentre.ca)*

Dave Jenkinson thinks a membership in the Canadian Children's Book Centre should be mandatory for all new parents, and I think I agree. One of the benefits of belonging is receiving *Children's Book News* on a quarterly basis. The magazine features news, reviews, biographies and other great ideas for using kids' books. You also receive *Our Choice*, the annual annotated catalogue of the best in Canadian children's books. Cost of a personal membership is $60.

Children's Literature Roundtables

The concept for CLRT was begun by UBC's Ron Jobe a couple of decades ago. Local children's literature enthusiasts band together and meet on an irregular basis to celebrate children's literature. Events include author talks and an annual voting for the CLRT non-fiction book for children, as well as participation in a joint project with the British Council, which sends out noted British authors for young people on tour in Canada. Cost to belong is nominal and the rewards are great for those who care about and value children's literature. If you don't have a Roundtable in your community, it would be well worth the effort to form one.

Kaleidoscope

Kaleidoscope is the grand old lady of children's and young adult literature conferences in Canada. Other conferences have fallen by the wayside, but Calgary teacher-librarians are planning to host the eighth edition in October 2004. Held every four years, the conference attracts the best in Canadian authors and an interesting contingent of international authors from the English-speaking world. It is a chance for all lovers of children's literature to connect and renew. A newer conference held every three years is Eastern Horizons. It is held in St. John's, Newfoundland, and celebrates Canadian writers and their works.

Resource Links

Vicki Pennell puts out our other reviewing journal for Canadian materials. This one is in print form and comes out every two months. Print form is always great to have around as you can slip the magazine into your bag and grab the highlighter wherever you are imprisoned (like the waiting room at the dentist) to note possibilities. *Resource Links* addresses the same titles as *CM*, and it is always valuable to be able to access a second viewpoint before considering whether you want to purchase something either personally or professionally. Vicki also provides a really good updating of book awards for children in Canada and a yearly index for all titles.

Thompson, Richard
Frog's Riddle and Other Draw-and-Tell Stories

Richard Thompson has devoted much of his career to creating stories that adults can draw and tell with children. The stories are easy to learn, usually humorous and painlessly expose children to the linear nature of narrative. Besides which, they are just a bunch of fun to share. My personal Thompson favorite, *Draw-and-Tell*, is out of print, but *Frog's Riddle* should be widely available.

Trelease, Jim (Editor) *Read All About It!*

While I learned a lot about children's literature from Jim Trelease's *Read-Aloud Handbook* and discovered a lot of must reads, the Trelease title that I use most in getting kids tuned in to books is *Read All About It!* Themed and very well put together, *Read All About It!* features excerpts from, and background material about, some of the great classics of children's literature. There is also room for some less well known but interesting work. It teases kids to do some personal exploration in their reading. It also covers a fairly large age range, right into the teenage years.

Part III: *Sally Bender*

Bouchard, David with Wendy Sutton *The Gift of Reading* ❧

It is not the job of the teacher or teacher-librarian to teach our kids to love reading. It is the job of the whole community. We are all in it together. That is the message of this book, which focuses on the active role that families, teachers, administrators must take if we are to give our children "the gift" that is a lifelong pleasure. The personal experiences of both authors give credence to the suggestions made for creating literate environments at home and school. Each provides a personal list of favorite books. What a great place to start. A wonderful resource for a children's literature class as well.

Butler, Dorothy *Babies Need Books: Sharing the Joy of Books with Children from Birth to Six*

For parents, teachers and librarians, or for any adult who wants to share the joy of books with young children, this book is a must. It includes Butler's guidelines for choosing appropriate books for children from birth to age six. She begins with good reasons for sharing books and provides a convincing argument using current brain research. Each chapter focuses on children as they grow and the importance of choice in the books being shared. Her lists are not long (too intimidating), and she has not included anything that she has not used with her own children and grandchildren. This book (in an earlier edition) set me on the road to many of the beliefs that I now hold about the inherent value of connecting children with books.

Although it is now out of print, *Cushla and Her Books*, Butler's story of the role that books played in the life of her handicapped granddaughter, is worth a search. If you are lucky, you will find it. Or you can borrow my copy.

Chambers, Aidan *The Reading Environment: How Adults Help Children Enjoy Books*

"Some people say they don't like reading stories, but I've never come across anyone who doesn't like hearing one." Aidan Chambers says we must create a reading environment that enables children to be willing, avid and thoughtful readers. Then he shows us how. In this short, easy read he offers advice that is practical for all and especially useful to remind us of things we may have forgotten as we meet the new challenges of the classroom. It is also valuable for less-experienced teachers to give guidance in establishing talk about books and a perfect place for reading them. He makes a strong point that reading aloud is necessary through all the school years. Hurrah!

Fox, Mem *Radical Reflections: Passionate Opinions on Teaching, Learning and Living*

Mem Fox feels that the enemy is "anything that keeps children from seeing reading and writing as sources of pleasure, growth and power in life." Using anecdotes and her trademark wit, Fox makes a case for helping children learn to care about language and the ways in which we can use it. She looks at a home that produces book lovers and notes that it has books in it, that the children have books of their own, that the variety of reading material is extensive, that children are allowed to read what interests them, that the parents love reading and that the books are delicious, rewarding and beautiful. These kids have parents who take their job seriously. This too would be a great resource for a children's literature class.

Fox, Mem *Reading Magic: Why Reading Aloud to Our Children Will Change Their Lives Forever*

In this chatty, informative book, Mem Fox regales us with personal stories that reflect the importance of reading aloud to all children. She says that we could change the face of illiteracy with three books a day and twenty minutes of reading between adult and child. She states emphatically that children need to have the advantage of the bonding and the love of language that this daily ritual ensures. Practical and easy to read, this is a perfect gift for new parents. Put it in a basket with some of your favorite books for the newborn.

What a treasure!

Harwayne, Shelley *Lasting Impressions*

I have often told friends that if I were teaching a children's literature course in a college or university, this would be my textbook. Shelley Harwayne and her staff at the Manhattan New School speak so passionately of the power of literature to enrich our lives. Her best advice comes on the first page: "Fill them up. Read aloud, read silently, recite, do choral readings, tell stories, dramatize, sing. Fill them up some more. Then step back and watch what happens." *Lasting Impressions* is an invaluable resource for all teachers. Harwayne shows what happens when we put fine literature into the hands of our children.

Kohl, Herbert *Should We Burn Babar?*

I love books that cause me to think in new and different ways and that stimulate my imagination. This book of essays, reports and observations does just that. It is not meant to preach but to raise our awareness. This book grew from a conversation that the author had with a caring and passionate teacher, who was finding that he stopped his students' talk about books because of the constraints of objectives and goals. His students were missing the opportunity to tell their stories and become engaged in meaningful dialogue, and he was becoming less effective as their mentor and guide. Kohl has always recognized stories as powerful tools for teaching and learning.

Pennac, Daniel *Better Than Life*

What happens between the time of warm and cozy bedtime rituals that include one story, or more, each evening and the independent adolescent who falls asleep trying to get through the first fifty pages of a Dickens novel on his own? Is it television? Is it hanging out at the mall? Electronic entertainment? Or is it that once our children learn to read on their own, we think we are getting back that fifteen minutes of freedom and we stop reading to them?

There are ways to get that joy back. It begins with the return to reading aloud. It insists that we stop asking questions at the end of every chapter. It requires that we give kids the time to read and let them learn again the pleasure. Ask nothing of them in return. This incredible book is filled with wisdom and deserves your attention.

Trelease, Jim *The Read-Aloud Handbook* (5th Edition)

I read this book after I heard the author speak to a large group of educators at a language arts conference in New Orleans. Powerful and dynamic, Trelease made point after point about the importance of reading with your kids. The first half of the book encourages turning off the TV and turning your kids on to books — a lifelong lesson that will bring daily pleasure. The second half is filled with a list of great books to read. I used his first edition as a guide when I was learning about literature, and I would have missed some wonderful books without his suggestions.

Wells, Gordon *The Meaning Makers:*
Children Learning Language and Using Language to Learn

If you are looking for research to bolster your notion that children's early read-aloud experiences have a lifelong impact, this is the book that you want to read. It is based on the Bristol Study, which was directed by the author. It followed a sample of thirty-two children from their first words through their elementary school years. Though the book is theoretical, it is interesting to meet the children and to read the transcripts of their language development. The study found that the single most important predictor of continued achievement in school was how much the children understood about literacy when they entered school. Their literacy was remarkably influenced by the number of books that had been read to them.

Part IV: *Lucie Poulin-Mackey*

Adams, Marilyn Jager, et al. *Conscience phonologique*
French text by Brigitte Stanké

If you are interested in phonemic awareness and its impact on young readers, this is the book for you, chock-full of practical ideas and exercises for the classroom. You will find different levels of difficulty, but most of all you will understand the chronological order in which things must progress in order to achieve maximum child language development. A-plus on my list.

Bedard, Denise and Danielle Montpetit
Stratégies . . . Stratégies pour une lecture efficace au primaire

A practical guide to help teachers help students use reading strategies to understand their reading. It also provides black-line masters to reproduce for evaluation purposes. An excellent guide.

Bombardier, Hélène and Pierre Elourdes
Le livre au cœur des apprentissages

A tool that will help the integration of subjects and is also fun for students. The authors propose an innovative way for students to be active in their learning through books. They also provide a CD-ROM with readings and activities that will help motivate all learners, especially those who may be at risk.

Chayer, Lucille Paquette *Compréhension de lecture*

This practical guide helps the teacher help the child discover the processes when trying to understand a passage. This approach helps children to organize their learning in different ways in order to retain information in their long-term memory. The author provides ideas for the teacher to become a guide in the child's learning.

Clay, Marie M. *Le sondage d'observation en lecture-écriture*

This book is written by the guru in the testing of literacy abilities. Marie Clay describes in detail a systematic way of observing and evaluating the child's progress in reading and writing. You will find normalized testing for the French-Canadian student population. A must for your collection

Courchesne, Danièle *Histoire de lire :*
La littérature jeunesse dans l'enseignement quotidien

This book provides insight on integrating children's literature into everyday teaching from French class to math to science. The author makes reference to activities that will help with developing strategies such as anticipation and the role of characters in the story. Plus she provides activities to integrate different genres of literature into a classroom setting. Some of the activities can be done in one lesson; others may take several days to complete. Black-line masters are available inside this useful book. A list of suggested readings is also available.

DeGaetano, Jean Gilliam (Editor) *De l'image à l'action*

This book is addressed to the young learner aged four to eight and helps with oral communication. The activities help the child develop basic comprehension skills and also build vocabulary. Speech therapists and parents will find this book useful.

Dore, Louise and Nathalie Michaud *Plaisir d'apprendre*

I used this book to create games for my grade one class. It contains activities for math, reading and writing—fun activities that teach as well. All the games are ready to print from the CD-ROM that accompanies the book. A fun resource.

Giasson, Jocelyne *La lecture : De la théorie à la pratique*

Jocelyne Giasson is a professor in the Faculty of Education at Laval University. Her many books are based on studies she has undertaken in the fields of language development and reading and writing. This is the most comprehensive book of theory I have encountered in my work. It will be useful not only to the beginner teacher but also to more experienced teachers. It is full of practical classroom applications. She has influenced many authors in their search for literacy excellence. You will also have great pleasure in reading her other book, *Les textes littéraires à l'école*. This one has even more practical ideas in it. Both should be in your personal professional library.

Nadon, Yves
Lire et écrire en première année et pour le reste de sa vie

In this book, Yves Nadon marries theory with practical ideas. Inspired by Jocelyne Giasson and many American reading gurus, Nadon explains in plain language his use of a balanced literacy program in his classroom, how it works and, more important, why it works. If you need a book that has both theory and practice, this is the book for you. It is by far my favorite in this field.

Stanké, Brigitte *L'apprenti lecteur*

This is another book of practical ideas for phonemic awareness. For the

Francophone population, *la conscience phonologique* implies more than just the study of phonics. Sentence structure, rhymes, syllable study, phonetics and letter recognition are all part of *la conscience phonologique*. If you are looking for a practical reference, this is your choice, filled with fun, reproducible activities for classroom use. You may also consult Stanké's other book, *Une phrase à la fois*, for strategies and activities that encourage oral communication.

St-Laurent, Lise, et al, *Lire et écrire à la maison : Programme de littératie familiale favorisant l'apprentissage de la lecture*

This book is addressed to teachers who want to help parents help their children with reading at home. This is an innovative approach involving parents in the school setting. Parents are asked to join the class and learn how their child learns to read through fun activities. The seminars end with a party in the school library. An excellent project to involve the community. You may also purchase five videos to supplement the book.

CHAPTER NINE

Do's and Don'ts

Part 1: *David Bouchard*

Do become addicted to books.

Do support your local and school library. And support your local bookstore. If literacy is important to you, show me the balance between books and technology in your homes and schools. Where are the books?

Do provide your children with lots of reading corners, the right chairs, lighting, book storage units, etc, in every appropriate spot in the home and school.

Do assure yourself that your children/students see you read.

Do talk books with your children and students, your friends and your colleagues.

Do make reading a sacred ritual — at least one special time each day.

Do seek out a multisensory approach to reading for all children.

Do make books accessible EVERYWHERE — in your homes, your cars, your . . .

Do surround yourself with your favorite books.

Do work at making your children believe they are readers — we are what we think we are.

Do not make reading a chore or a punishment. "After supper, you'll do the dishes, read for half an hour and then you can go play." Instead try . . . "After supper, you'll do the dishes, go play for half an hour and then you can read."

Do not bribe your children to read (i.e., readathons are not in the best interest of developing readers).

Do not DAM the pleasure out of reading anything, particularly poetry. DAM stands for the Dissecting, Analyzing and Meaningless Memorizing that children are too often asked to do.

Do not test the pleasure out of reading. We in North America are and have been on the road to disaster for what seems to be forever as we test our children, often as early as grade three and sometimes even earlier. Ask any teacher to find out if this ever-growing obsession with testing isn't killing the desire to read that we should be trying to ignite in our children. Of course it is. Our babies are stressed. They are frightened to death. The reason we want them to read is much softer and more spiritual than achievement. We want them to discover a means of intimately understanding others and the world around them . . . and eventually of being able to share the same. We want to offer our babies a place to rest and, on occasion, a place to hide (i.e., 9/11). We want them to be able to access the world of so many others in what has proven to be the most personal and intimate manner possible: through the written word.

Do not delegate reading to one parent or to a single teacher. Mom was never meant to be the only person who would read to the children. Nor should she be the only one to do the vacuuming.

Do not label a child a weak or reluctant reader. This type of labeling does nothing to encourage a child to read. Reading readiness does not come at a specific age. For some it comes as early as kindergarten; for others, much later.

Do not ever think that any child can or should be considered a "standard" child. Give no credence to standardized reading tests. The plethora of standardized tests that has a death grip on this continent is doing NO GOOD whatsoever at getting North America reading. Quite the contrary. It is having a disastrous effect in our schools and in our homes. And even for the children to whom we are giving the tools to read, we are not giving them the heart.

Do not rule out light, fun reading. Do not attempt to cut comics, magazines, easy and light reading out of the lives of your children. There are many adults whose reading consists almost exclusively of "light" material. These adults are literate and love reading as much as those who read nothing but the classics. (As a funny aside, my wife, Vicki, is lying in bed at my side as I write, soaking up every word and picture in this month's issue of *English Garden*.)

Do not overly censor your child's reading.

Do not use phonics as a first approach to teaching children how to read. Phonics does serve a purpose, but remember that children learn to read just as they learn to walk and talk.

Part II: *Anne Letain*

Do try to expose kids to the right book at the right time. The first and maybe only consideration when selecting a book to share with children is the book's ability to create an emotional connection. Children need books that allow them to look inside themselves and to grow as individuals and also as contributors to the society that they inhabit. Great literature provides children with points of illumination and self-reflection and participation in their world. It is far too easy to read the back of the book and see if it is leveled by age or grade or to check if its content is appropriate for use in social studies or science or life skills. These are not the most important criteria.

Do remember that children and adults look at books with two completely different sets of lenses — unfortunately, adults bring an inordinate amount of experiential baggage and "grown-ups know best" thinking to the books they feel children should read. Often kids are fresher and more open minded about books and are as entitled to their own opinions as adults are. Prior to leading a discussion on *The Tulip Touch* by Anne Fine, a group of my students wanted to offer a prayer for Tulip and Natalie, the two troubled lead characters in the book.

Do remember the gender gap. Boys are far pickier about what they wish to read and in general respond well to action, humor and high fantasy. Girls are more generous and eclectic in their reading choices. They will read what boys read, but the reverse is not necessarily true.

Do share your personal enthusiasm for reading with kids. Don't hesitate to pick favorite parts in books and use them as "teasers" for kids. This is a simple way to pull along the most reluctant consumer of print.

Do check up on your kids' and students' reading. My students are expected to tell me what they are currently reading. This is not the reading police, and my students really do like to tell me about what they are reading. Interestingly, in true practical kid style, they usually have two books on the burner at any one time — one for school and one for home. And it's still a shock when some small human cannonball hits me at Costco with the news "I'm already on chapter eight of *Holes*."

Do try to accept that *Love You Forever* is not really a kids' book despite its best-seller status. It is really a book for adults, and it is not the only adult book disguised as a book for children — beware of these books in sheep's clothing! Still not a believer? Try reading *Love You Forever* to a group of seven-year-olds.

Do provide opportunities where kids and their parents can purchase books. Many communities do not have a bookstore, so the school book fair is an excellent venue for book ownership by kids. When an author visits a school, make sure students have an opportunity to buy the author's books at reasonable cost. Also, make sure there are appropriate occasions to gift children with books such as birthdays, awards or draws.

Do consider providing the children in your life with magazines in their own names — a birthday gift at reasonable cost that just keeps on giving!

Do encourage kids to talk to each other about what they are reading or to do tandem reading of the same book. Adults are not the only arbiters of a good read.

Do give kids a chance to meet and connect with real live authors. It is important for them to know and understand that a real person created the book they've read — and it's also a great stimulus for them to understand the power of ideas and imagination.

Don't ruin the flow of a story while you are reading it to children. Educators are often guilty of stopping a story regularly to check for comprehension and vocabulary. We forget that listening is an important life skill, and that there is a certain joy that comes from listening.

Don't be offended by "gross" in kids' books. Children have a natural affinity for bodily functions and secretions and will generally get over this fascination without too much adult intervention. Why not just enjoy *Walter the Farting Dog*? Or the maggot scene in *Jack's Black Book*? Or the opening scenario of *Bumface*? Childhood should have some plain old fun about it. Never underestimate the power of *Captain Underpants*!

Don't forget that the picture book can be a conduit to the whole world of literature. The *I Spy*-type books can be excellent entry points to getting kids excited about books in general. Why not follow up with Graeme Base's *Animalia* or Michael Rosen's *ABC* or *Alphabet City*? *Round Trip* and *It Looked Like Spilt Milk* are gimmick books with high appeal to kids. And a great pop-up can never go amiss, either.

Don't forget that the public library often has a plethora of free or nearly free programs for babies and up (in age) that promote an interest in reading. Where most children's activities today cost an arm and a leg, these programs are affordable, and children can reap rich rewards as they discover the delights of the public library. I come from a family where you only bought something if you could eat it, and the public library is largely the reason that I am a reader today.

Don't let a book get stale for you. Unless you can stay enthusiastic about sharing a particular book with kids, it is better for both the child and the adult to move on to something new and different and exciting for both parties.

Don't overlook movie and media tie-ins. There are many excellent discussions waiting to happen as kids compare favorite books to the movies that they have inspired. Conversely, kids who have been watching Franklin, Clifford, Arthur and Elliot on television will actively seek out the books in the school library. Again, it's just another route into reading.

Lunch with the Boys

For the past two years, I have been hosting and directing Oprah-style book discussion groups with the students in my school. In various permutations and combinations (by gender, grade, cross grade, with or without other adults, with guest leaders, etc.), we have now completed nineteen discussions or Grand Conversations, as we call them. Participation in the Grand Conversation is always voluntary on the part of the kids, but demand to continue the "talk" remains unabated.

Without question, it is the boys-only (nine- and ten-year-olds) discussion groups that have provided me with the most cause for reflection and the most laughs. After all, it is not too often that a distinctly middle-aged female teacher gets to be an honorary boy.

First, there's the eating part. For those who've been through the parenting cycle, this part of the process is akin to sharks at a feeding frenzy or a birthday party on steroids. You cannot provide too much food, and it is gone in a whisper, or is that a roar? Invariably there is discussion on whether I ordered the pizza from the right place, and at least one pop can will be crushed to smithereens before I can point out that the activity better not be contagious. At one Grand Conversation, after the boys had inhaled a couple of dozen sodas, five large pizzas, a large sack of quartered oranges and three dozen cookies, one intrepid soul brought out an institutional-sized can of Zoodles and his personal Swing-a-Matic can opener. They only disappeared after he received "the look" and had the good sense to return the items sheepishly to his knapsack.

Recently, the boys (grade four) and I, fifteen strong, met to talk about *Jack's Black Book*. This is part of a quartet of semi-autobiographical and hilarious books by Jack Gantos about the years he was in grades five, six, seven and eight. Gantos is an award-winning American author with a unique view of the middle years. Although kids seem to have no problem with his memories of a childhood growing up in Florida, some parents do not find his work quite so appealing. One dad called to let me know that the book was disgusting; even so, his twin sons were the first through the door to discuss it.

So, as I mentioned in Chapter Four, to begin this particular Conversation, I read part of a book review by an adult who did not find Jack's antics too entertaining either, and who had ended the revie, "Not recommended." My boys were almost universally incensed and offended. Didn't the reviewer know that boys like "gross"? One imaginative participant decided that the book could be described as "vomitrocious"; a word I think should be considered for the next edition of the *Oxford Canadian Dictionary*.

Over time, my students have developed a kind of protocol for the discussions. Those present can offer up questions in two formats: questions that can be responded to by anyone, and questions that must travel around the table to be answered by everyone (including me). The boys direct this second sort of question with a military precision born of much experience with organized sport and coaching. We have designated "starters," designated direction, and no one is permitted to pass on the question.

For *Jack's Black Book*, the boys introduced this series of round-the-table questions, which I think reflects their high involvement with the book. First, What was your favorite part of the book? Then, What is your favorite worst part of the book? Then, What part of the book didn't you get? And finally, What is the coolest part of the book? Needless to say, the boys' observations were wonderful — enlightened, perceptive and funny — and a credit to how thoroughly they had read the book.

The lunch hour most often ends with the boys wanting to know what we are going to tackle next. As time has passed, the boys have taken a larger personal interest in what they would like to read and talk about. I often find grubby pieces of paper on my workspace or stickies affixed to my computer bearing suggestions for the next read. It is truly encouraging to note that the boys want books with some meat to them, usually works of fantasy and high adventure.

When I have suggested that we trash the "boys only" concept and return to mixed groups, the boys are adamant — no girls except by special dispensation! According to the lads it's because girls "yap" too much and like girly books. And as a teacher with many rings on her trunk, I tend to agree that girls of the same age are inclined to be more verbal and therefore to dominate group discussion.

So if your life has been lacking that little extra lately or needs an infusion of energy, why not consider lunch with the boys and a book? You'll get some food if you're fast, guaranteed excitement, and you might even learn a thing or five from all that youthful testosterone!

Grand Conversations or book discussion groups need not be limited in any way — in terms of who takes part or when or where. Since I began the concept we have done groups as small as ten and groups as large as twenty-five. We have done girls-only, boys-only and parent-and-child groups. We have done doubles — two books together on the same theme — and we have used challenging kids' books for the three times we have done staff discussion groups. These, of course, usually involve a flagon of wine or two. But I think the best part of the Grand Conversations for both young and old is that there is no homework or book report, and you are only there at the discussion because you want to be!

Part III: *Sally Bender*

Do read a great book without showing the illustrations, and let kids create their own settings and characters as they listen. Then read the book showing the pictures, and talk about how their perceptions compared to the author's and illustrator's vision for the same story. Why?

Do make time during each school day to read one picture book, one poem and one chapter from the novel being read to the class . . . or more.

Do use variety in the voices of the changing characters to pique interest and add drama. This inspires kids to do the same when they are reading on their own or to others. They need us to be active and inspiring models for them.

Do be sure that you have read the books yourself that you are going to read out loud, and only read the ones that you love. There are so many to be savored and loved that you will never run out of books to share.

Do try an author/illustrator study when you notice that your listeners are really connected to the work of one person. Read all the books that they have published. Check the Internet for additional information. Many authors have their own web sites, and you might even have a chance to hear them read from their work or to send an e-mail with questions and comments. This type of integrated study allows kids to spend extra time with an artist who inspires them, or an author whose words touch their hearts.

Do choose the right questions. A good question to ask if you have finished reading a wonderful new book to a group is, Who has something to share? This gives listeners the opportunity to put their thoughts into words and allows conversations to begin.

Do look for books that excite, intrigue and entertain your own particular listeners. If they have a special interest, take the time to find books that will enhance their love of the subject and expand on that fascination.

Do provide time to respond, space to relax and encouragement to develop new passions.

Do make sure that kids have frequent opportunities to visit your local library, school library and bookstore to browse and savor books that appeal to their own sensibilities and interests.

Do model your love and enthusiasm for reading . . . day and night, weekdays and weekends, on the hammock or in the bathtub, in silent delight or raucous pleasure. Kids need models and they deserve the best!

Don't make readers finish books that they are not enjoying. You don't finish books you don't enjoy, do you?

Don't talk about every single book you share. Sometimes kids need time to think over what they have heard and what they thought about while they were listening.

Don't give them a task as a follow-up for every book. We don't write book reports each time we read a new book.

Don't reward kids for reading. Let reading be its own reward. I detest those programs that offer kids food for reading books. As one good friend suggested, Wouldn't it be better if the restaurant offered kids a book for eating their fare? What a splendid idea!

Don't stop reading to your children once they can read on their own. We tend to forget the pleasure of listening to a well-read story enjoyed together. We often stop reading when our children become independent, and we lose an amazing bonding time.

Don't read anything to them that you do not like yourself. Kids are so perceptive and will soon recognize your displeasure with the task at hand. There are many wonderful books to read; just keep looking until you find the ones that you love too.

Don't read only those books that your children choose. I read *Goodnight Moon* by Margaret Wise Brown 1,678 times and I loved it too, but it was not the only book that we read each night. The kids chose one, and we chose one or two. This ensures that you keep introducing them to the pleasures of many books and many genres.

Don't punish children by taking away their story time. Bad behavior will not be eliminated when you threaten children with the loss of the time that you spend together sharing brilliant stories and poetry. Aren't you also punishing yourself?

Don't make children choose between television and reading. It is the job of the adults to establish bedtime routines. The television is turned off at a certain time, and then there is time for reading. If the child chooses not to read, that is fine. Lights out!

Don't limit children's choices in reading. They need to sample many books in order to determine what speaks to their hearts and to their minds. If we make all choices for them, how will they come to know the real pleasure that can be found in a well-chosen book?

Part IV: *Lucie Poulin-Mackie*

Do read to your children on a daily basis or as often as possible. The bond that you will create will be permanent. You will show your child how reading works and share hours of reading pleasures. If you only have a few minutes to spend with your children, try to make it time to share a book. That is time well invested for the rest of their lives.

Don't use your reading time as a punitive measure. Don't take away reading time if you need to take away a privilege from your children. Take away other things but not reading.

Do read a variety of genres to your children. Share magazine articles, recipes, letters, newspaper articles, cereal boxes and more. They need to understand that reading has purpose and form and it can also be fun.

Don't limit the genres that they are exposed to, including the Internet. Just be aware of the material they are reading.

Do read the same story over and over again if asked to. Children create emotional bonds with stories, songs, poems, movies and sayings. They may love the story line, the play with language or other features. They will learn language structure through repetition.

Don't pretend. Children sense our emotions and will lose interest if we don't show them that we enjoy reading. If you are not a reader, tell your child; be honest. They have a right not to like reading, but ask them why they don't and try to encourage them to become readers. Reading is, after all, the doorway to the world.

Do make time to read as well. You are the best model for your children no matter how old they are. Take time for yourself and share your reading with your children. When we've read a good book, we often talk about it. We want our children to become well-rounded adults; let's show them how.

Don't judge your child's reading materials. It can be hard to make our children read once they reach a certain age. If they are reading, encourage it. Don't judge it unless it is immoral or dangerous to their health.

Do offer your child help if he or she is having difficulty reading. See the teacher and ask what can be done at home to help.

Don't give the answer automatically if your children cannot read a word. Ask them to use cues to help them read the word. Look at the picture, separate the word into syllables, look for the small word in the big word, for example. If after a few seconds the child has not read the word, you may then offer help.

Do praise your child's reading. They will become fluent readers. An action that is praised will be repeated.

Do have fun. Reading with your child is time well invested for their future.

Index of Titles

Index of Authors

Acknowledgements

No one will have worked harder on this than our knowledgeable and capable editor. Thank you, Maggie, for your ways and wisdom.

— *David Bouchard*

Where would we be without those who share our books? Thanks . . . to my school kids through the years who have listened, and talked and asked for more. And thanks to my friend David who honors my opinions and invited me to join him on this lovely project.

— *Sally Bender*

An especial thank you to David for the invitation to work on this project, but much gratitude as well to Sally, Lucie and Maggie for making the whole endeavor such a rewarding experience.

— *Anne Letain*

A chance meeting years ago has brought me to what I really want to do, write books. Thank you, David, for giving me the opportunity to work with you and to share my love of reading. Your kind words of wisdom have made me believe even more deeply that good books are the foundation of a good literacy program.

Thank you, Anne and Sally. Your profound love of children and reading has inspired me. Although distances separate us, our mutual love of books and bringing them to readers has brought us close.

Thank you, Maggie. Your encouraging words have helped me through the process in this, my first professional writing endeavor.

Thank you, Mom, for reading *Green Eggs and Ham* to me every night in your broken English.

— *Lucie Poulin-Mackey*

DAVID BOUCHARD was a non-reader until adulthood. He fell in love with children's books one day when he was asked to read a chapter of a novel aloud to a class. He lives in Victoria, British Columbia.

SALLY BENDER is a teacher-librarian who writes a book review column for the *Brandon Sun*. She lives in Brandon, Manitoba.

ANNE LETAIN is a teacher-librarian, a consultant and the host of the web site, The Read Aloud Registry. She lives in Coaldale, Alberta.

LUCIE POULIN-MACKEY has been a teacher for almost twenty years. She is now a literacy specialist for her French school board. She lives in Guelph, Ontario.